# ABUELITA I AM YOUR GRANDSON

# ABUELITA
# I AM YOUR
# GRANDSON

## JULIO LUCERO

FIRST EDITION

Cover design, interior by Barış Şehri
Photo by Lyle Lovett

Library of Congress Cataloging-in-Publication Data has been applied for.

One story in this collection has appeared elsewhere, in slightly different form: "Milpero" in Oddball Magazine

# Contents

# Chismógrafo

Asti had just finished their new patio. It was the talk of the neighborhood and filled up fast. Our patio had no buzz. I reassured myself that dinner time was approaching, and soon we'd be busy, too. Meanwhile, we were killing time. The lavatrastes had no dishes to wash, so she was hanging out by the window. We watched someone with an expensive-looking camera snap photos of the neighborhood and Asti's bustling patio. "Allí va el chismógrafo," the lavatrastes said. There goes a gossiper. I thought the comment was clever and insightful.

Which brings me to a crucial juncture. I'm not here to chismear, to gossip, or spread rumors. Instead, I'm here to share snapshots of memories that rest on a foundation of personal experiences and perspectives. I've changed the names of the people I mention and randomly changed their genders to protect their identities.

# Prologue

Mom got the restaurant in the divorce. She had a few years of experience under her belt, and when she realized what she needed to learn, it was too late to turn back. I knew I had to get involved. What followed were thirteen years of wild success.

One day, after a particularly rough week, when I was about to begin my shift, Mom approached me, glanced around to make sure no one was listening, and said, "I'm selling the restaurant."

This is not a woman who acts on impulse. Her words don't flop around like a trout desperate for the gulf. I knew she had thought this through.

But there was a problem. Selling a restaurant isn't the same as posting a La-Z-Boy recliner on Craigslist. And what would the family say? The community? Our customers? It was more than I could process. Emotions, history, business, money, family— I felt as if a hippo had landed on my plate. But the most difficult part? I couldn't talk to anyone about it. Bottling up all of those emotions wouldn't work. I needed a way to talk without anyone listening.

I began to write.

# The Shoulds

When I met people at parties or social gatherings, and they discovered that I worked in the family restaurant, one of the many questions they asked, if not the first, was what I did at the café. It was a fair question, because, as the owner's son, I could have done anything. I could have been another busser or runner, possibly a manager, or even the head tequila taster.

On a more serious note, I used to struggle when people asked that question. Contrary to what many might think, working in the family business isn't straightforward. I wasn't the owner or a regular employee. What I did varied. When I was younger and free of grown-up responsibility, my tasks were mostly physical and in the face of customers. As I got older, I gradually took on more administrative duties. And if I may add, administrative work is the pits of restaurant work, the pits of any job, really. More than drinking or smoking or staying out late at night, nothing will age a young soul faster than the tedium of a spreadsheet.

I yearn to be young and spreadsheet-free again. That is, for the most part, because there's one thing I don't miss about being a young owner's son, not even in the slightest. And that's the shoulds.

The staff don't get the shoulds. They have little say in how the business operates. The owner, Mom, had a say in the business, but very few individuals had the cojones to give her the shoulds treatment. As the still-young son of the owner, I was the bouncer who got all the shoulds – shoulds that should have fallen on Mom and the workers landed squarely on me.

Say a customer walks in, grabs a menu and scans it up and down, turns it around and around again, looking for something he can't find. Finally, he looks up at me, "I see chicken enchiladas, but I don't see beef enchiladas."

"We only serve chicken enchiladas and cheese enchiladas."

"No beef enchiladas?" The split on his brow deepens. "What kind of Mexican restaurant is this?"

"Sorry about that. We mostly focus on chicken dishes."

"Y'all should consider serving beef enchiladas, y'all'd make more money." And just like that, I was hit with a should and a would, a classic one-two combination like a prizefighter following his jab with a hook or a cross. One two, jab cross, should, would.

Or the lady asking about menudo. "You don't make menudo?"

"No, we only have caldo de pollo."

"Not even on the weekends?"

"Sorry."

"You should add menudo to your menu. It's hard to find a good menudo around here."

"No mezcal? You'd kill it if you added a mezcal-rita." Should.

"No crunchy tacos?" Another should.

The shoulds don't come from callousness or a place of ill intention. On the contrary, they often come from people who mean well. Which somehow made them worse. As the saying goes, the road to hell is paved with good intentions. And if I may add, a road laid with one should at a time.

From the customer's perspective, giving the shoulds to the owner's son made total sense. However, as the owner's young son,

I couldn't act on the shoulds. I lacked the power and authority to execute their suggestions. That's the thing about being the owner's son. Before taking on managerial and administrative duties, the son has to put in his time learning the ropes of the business, bouncing and checking the shoulds at the door. It isn't until much later, if ever, that the owner's kin is granted the authority to make business decisions. And again, because it begs to be stated once more: if ever.

One night after closing, I went down the street to a beer garden to meet up with some friends. After grabbing a pint at the bar, I went outside to look for them. I saw them across the patio, and I walked towards them. Halfway down, I heard someone call out my name. "Julio." I looked over. It was the young couple from two doors down. They'd just opened a cheese shop and were the newest addition to the corner. I stopped and said hello. As we chatted, one of them said, "Julio, y'all should totally..." something something. I can't remember what the should was, only that there was a should. Immediately after the should was stated, the non-should-er gently reminded the should-er how much they disliked hearing the shoulds from other people. As if to say, "Babe, you shouldn't say should."

To my surprise, these two were founders and owners of a business, yet they also got the shoulds. It wasn't just me. More than likely, Mom and Aunt Bobbie must get the shoulds, too. And back in the day, Papá must have gotten them. However, I think it's safe to assume they didn't get the same concentration of shoulds I did. I say this because as I've gotten older, the shoulds have diminished as if it were indirectly correlated with age. The older you were, the fewer shoulds you received.

I don't miss being bombarded by shoulds. I'll swap them out for the rows and columns of a spreadsheet any day. Take the señora that recently came in. She scanned the menu and asked if we served caldo de res, beef soup. "We only have caldo de pollo. It's really popular, though." She looked at the menu for just a few seconds longer. "I'm really craving caldo de res. I'll come back when I want the pollo." She returned the menu, turned around, and left.

On the surface her action seemed harsh, but not that bad either. Not for an adult, at least. Rejection seems fair and natural, leaps and bounds better than the señora dishing out a should.

# Bouncing and Bound

There is no shortage of reasons why I admire children. Near the top of my list are how quickly they pick up language and how imaginative they can be. As a child, we made games out of anything. Just walking on the sidewalk with my best bud became a game. "Step on a crack and break your mother's back!" he shouted, hopping over cracks. "Step on a line and break your mother's spine!" I countered, leaping over lines.

One of the things I adored about games of the imagination was how well they traveled. We played the game of lines and cracks on the blacktop during recess, on tennis courts, and in the hallway walking to the school cafeteria. I even played at home on my own, making my way from one side of the kitchen to the other, tiptoeing on only the center of the tiles. Some of the best tiles were the black and white vinyls at the café. The checkered pattern was like a chess board, with chairs and tables adding to the challenge.

We started on the tiles in the dining room and migrated to other areas of the restaurant, such as the kitchen, dish pit, and office, oblivious of the people working. Sometimes, tiles or no tiles, I got bored and wandered around the restaurant as if I owned the place. I rambled into the kitchen, then over to the dish pit, until I arrived at the back office, which was an adventure more than a destination. There was nothing in the office an eight-year-old might find interesting. I returned to the dining room the same way I came, through the dish pit and past the cooks working in the kitchen.

"Papi, stay out of the kitchen," Mom and Aunt Bobbie would say. "They're working. We don't want you to burn yourself." I heard what they told me but kept on. Back and forth I went, to and from the office and through the sweaty kitchen, until one of the workers got fed up and griped about me being in the way. Tiles or no tiles, the restaurant was not a playground. "Go outside and play."

I gravitated to the trees between the sidewalk and the street. The mulberry had a complex root pattern at its trunk, resembling a mangled web. I stepped on the roots and strummed the jagged bark with the tips of my fingers as I circumnavigated the tree. This time, I played Lava, inspired by the game we played on the playscape. The goal was simple: loop around the tree without veering off the roots and onto the volcanic ground. Otherwise, you were toast.

After a few goes, the lava game became a snore, so I added scenes from my favorite cartoon, X-Men. Now, I was Wolverine, my favorite hero. I raged and mauled robot Sentinels with my claws and pulled out their sparking electrical wires like a toddler playing with spaghetti. Next, I became another hero, Nightcrawler, whose superpower was teleportation. I teleported everywhere, sporadically and randomly, which disoriented the Sentinels. When Nightcrawler confused them, I turned into Gambit and threw kinetically charged cards at them. As my mind phased in and out of superhero scenes, my feet stayed on the roots, safely above the lava below.

From then on, whenever we went to the café, I played on the roots of one of my favorite trees. I destroyed Sentinels in the most elaborate ways a third grader could. Inevitably, the games became a snooze. For them to work, my imagination had to be firing on every cylinder, and after a while, no amount of mental calculus could keep me occupied.

One evening, Mom was taking extra-long at the café. I was done with the lava, and I couldn't fabricate another Sentinel to destroy. I dug deep and recalled an action movie I'd seen Papá watching one evening. This time, the hero was James Bond. Like the X-Men, Bond was always finding trouble and somehow always managed to wiggle out of it. The best trick he ever pulled off was when he was trapped on a rock surrounded by crocodile-infested waters. In a series of cat-like moves, he skipped on the backs of the crocs, in one sequence after the next, like a flat rock bouncing on a still pond. Bond's escape was beyond anything a human could do—anyone but me, of course.

While Mom was inside, I practiced for my future career as a double agent. An array of picnic tables was lined up outside, and I pretended they were crocs. I stepped onto the first table and leaped from table to table all the way across the patio. "I made it!" I thought. "I escaped the crocs and made it to the other side!"

Once wasn't enough. If I were going to be like Bond, I'd have to practice. This time, after the third table, I leaped back onto the middle table and then back to the first. I turned around and did it again and again until Mom saw me from the window and came out to scold me. Her words didn't stick. Not more than a couple of minutes after she went back inside, I began hurtling across the tables again. Nothing could keep me from becoming the best Bond the world had ever seen. Croc one to croc two, to three to two to one, over and over again.

When I opened my eyes, my peripheral vision was blurry and dim. My legs were over my body, and my face was pressed against the picnic table bench. I saw my teeth on the bench and screamed, then began to cry.

It took me a moment to get to my feet. The pain was so acute it commanded my full attention. The entrance to the restaurant was just a few yards away. I pushed the front door open and made my way past the register into the kitchen. No one was there. I thought they must be in the restroom, which was in the opposite corner. I stumbled by a few booths with patrons and let my mouth drape so they could see how bloody it was. I wanted the world to see what I did.

Aunt Bobbie was in the restroom with Marisa. When she saw my mouth, she immediately began rinsing it with water. As I whooshed water in my mouth, I finally worked up the courage to strum my tongue against my teeth. There was a gap on the bottom row, two throbbing sockets where teeth should have been. The thought of missing teeth was worse than the pain.

Mom had been at the store. When she got back, she darted outside and searched for my teeth. My teeth were still on the bench, perfectly intact. A family friend told her they should be placed in milk. Not a minute later, we are rushing to St. David's hospital, my two teeth floating in a cup of milk.

My head was tilted back, my jaw agape, and the hospital lights were blinding. I was surrounded by nurses and a doctor. Papá was there, too. Mom couldn't watch. She had to step away. The doctor was fussy because I was crying, but managed to wedge the roots back into their tender sockets. Setting my teeth back in place was excruciating, much worse than having them knocked out.

When we left the hospital, Mom didn't head home but drove in the opposite direction to our dentist's office. My vision had returned to normal, and my hard tears had dwindled to soft sobs. My injury didn't faze Dr. Hassle. He looked in my mouth and calmed me. He said everything would be fine and told Mom to bring me to the office first thing in the morning.

The next morning, Dr. Hassle installed a thin metal wire along my lower teeth. I'd seen kids at school with braces, but mine were less extensive.

Within weeks, my teeth settled back into their sockets. Dr. Hassle's work had been so precise I had no visible signs I'd been injured. But I'd left teeth-shaped indentations in the wooden bench. And a third tooth had been chipped and was sensitive. To this day, I don't bite into ice cream.

The most evident reminder of my fall, however, wasn't physical. The trauma from the fall was so significant that it forever affected my relationship with my imagination, and I avoided daring activities, such as skateboarding and other extreme sports.

My career as a hotshot double agent never materialized. Nor did any future dreams of becoming the next Tony Hawk or Jackie Chan. To this day, I've noticed a fissure between my physical coordination and imagination. I still ride a bike, but my body is grounded with the tiles, cracks, and lines. Thankfully, my imagination still soars safely over the crocs and bounces over molten lava.

# Potatoes, Tomatoes, Avocados, Orange Juice

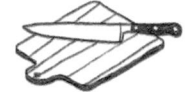

Growing up in the '90s was the epitome of being carefree. When I was a kid, the Earth's pull and the overwhelming gravity of modern politics and current events didn't seem so heavy. I'm sure Mom and my tías would argue that the era when they grew up was the last hoorah, and the generation before theirs would probably also say they were the last generation with an untainted childhood. But let me slip in real quick that I think you had it okay, so long as your childhood was slightly dull. Intermittent bouts of boredom made for a wonderful childhood.

With that said, I'm not advocating for an insipid childhood. Instead, I want to highlight what we did to escape that, especially during the summer. We still had a handful of years before the internet gripped us, so we had to be resourceful. We were regular fliers at Garrison Park, our neighborhood pool, and bicycles were part of the equation. I thumbed our poor Gameboy until the machine, and I both went dim. We often visited our friends a few houses down to jump on their trampoline like wild goats. Even when they were away on vacation, we'd sneak in.

Two and a half months of summer vacation was an eternity, and our luxuries didn't take long to become redundant. We begged for more batteries and sped up and down the street on our bikes until we'd memorized every crack and divot. No matter what we did, we were bored out of our minds. In desperation, I made Mom and Papá a proposal. I wanted to work in the café. They'd said no when I'd asked before, but this time, they said yes.

When Papá went to work in the morning, I tagged along. We were silent in the car on the way there. I looked out the passenger window nearly the entire time. After all the Saturday morning garage sales Mom dragged us to, I knew my way around town, not by street names but landmarks.

We entered the cafè through the backdoor, and Ximena, the planchera, greeted us. Then, I took an apron from the bin by the door, looped the top part around my neck, reached around my back, and grappled with the lengthy strings. Ximena saw me fumbling, she wrapped the strings around my paunchy waist. A firm tug and a tight knot later, I was ready for my shift.

On my first day, Ximena showed me the basics. She taught me to make salsitas, to-go salsas. Then she showed me how to peel potatoes and dice tomatoes. When an order was ready, I ran the food. When customers left, I bussed the table. I was shown how to prepare chickens for the rotisserie. I loved ripping out the fatty pieces before putting them on the skewer. Next to the prep area was the dish pit. The lavatrastes was all smiles. He finally had company. He said something to me in Spanish, but I didn't have an inkling what it meant. Spanish was my native tongue, but I forgot nearly every syllable once I started school.

After we prepped the chickens and set the skewers in the rotisserie, Ximena asked, "Papi, tienes hambre?" She repeated her question in English. Are you hungry? Hambre was one of the few Spanish words I remembered. I was always hambre. It was still morning, so breakfast tacos were the obvious choice. The question was, what did

I want my tacos made with? Chorizo, potatoes, eggs, cheese ... nothing fancy, a classic combination. I was still at the age when Mom called the shots on the foods we ate. She said chorizo was too greasy, something about lymph nodes. I had zero idea what lymph nodes were, but if that's what made chorizo so delicious, give me the lymph nodes. Mom wasn't there. She didn't have to know.

In no time, Ximena whipped up a couple of sizable chorizo tacos, and I scurried to the booth in the corner by the restrooms. The cocinero and lavatrastes came to visit and bantered in Spanish. I could make out "gordito." I knew that meant chubby. But they said it in a tone of voice that wasn't shaming. If anything, it was endearing. The rest of their chatter was a mystery.

Eventually, they realized my Spanish was zero and went back to work. Being Hispanic without knowing Spanish pressed. I was too timid to learn Spanish, unable to claim my parents' identity.

One day, Papá had a bone to pick on the way to work. He wanted me up front with the customers, not in the back peeling potatoes. "That's the cocineros' job," he said. "Your job is to be up front with the customers. Ask them if they want more coffee or more water. Bullshit with them."

Even at ten, eleven years old, I kind of knew what bullshitting was: lots of words, more than necessary, and usually more fun amongst adults. Bullshitting and Spanish were oddly similar. They were easy to spot, sometimes tricky to understand, and nearly impossible to replicate. Or as others would say, including me: "I kind of understand it, but I can't speak it."

It seemed to me then that Papá was a decent bullshitter, but as an adult, I realized he was quite gifted at it, or at least well-practiced. His Spanish accent was entertainment in itself, and he had a non-native perspective, often coupling things and ideas in ways others wouldn't connect, two qualities that lent themselves perfectly to the art of bullshitting.

When I got to work, I didn't go up front as Papá had asked but stayed in the back with the tomatoes and potatoes. Between not knowing how to bullshit with the customers and not knowing Spanish, I choose to be with the crew. Ximena made a great point. "You have to learn this in case you don't have anyone helping you one day." I took that to heart and began honing my peeling and dicing skills. It helped that there was a space in my preadolescent mind gratified by peeling and dicing. And I liked being part of a crew, out of the house, working with adults. Compared to the blahs of summer, working at the café was better any day.

It bugged Papá that I always looked out the passenger window as we drove to work. And it irritated him more that I was still spending so much time prepping in the back. He didn't see that I was learning the business from the ground up. He thought I was being manipulated. The potatoes and tomatoes, "that is their work," he repeated. "They are paid to do that!"

When we got to work, he took me straight to the front counter and showed me how the cash register worked. The breakfast items were listed in the left column, and the à la carte items, chalupas, too, were in the middle columns. The lunch and dinner plates were to the right.

Three buttons were particularly important. The first was the "extra ingredient" button, located next to the breakfast taco button. If a breakfast taco had more than three ingredients, I had to push that button for every extra ingredient. The next button was the avocado button, little explanation needed. The last, and probably most crucial, button was the orange juice button. "If someone orders an orange juice, charge them for an orange juice." He paused. "If that person comes up and wants a refill, charge them for another orange juice." He paused again. "I don't care what anyone says ... *no* free refills."

The next day, or maybe the day after, Papá reminded me again that there were *no* free orange juice refills and revealed the price of a gallon. He bought the juice freshly squeezed from a local company called Good Flow. It wasn't until many years later that it was realized that distributing unpasteurized juice was considered perilous to public health and prohibited.

One morning, Papá had something else going on and couldn't give me a ride to work, so Mom gave me a ride instead. I wasn't so soft-spoken with her. For most of the commute, I bellyached about not wanting to go to the restaurant. Working at the café had lost its luster. What had begun as a new adventure had become mundane. I wanted my humdrum summer back.

"You'll feel better after work," Mom replied. "I always feel better after work than I do before work," she nudged, not letting me off the hook so easily.

Work went as usual, without any sensational events or happenings. Later that afternoon, when Mom picked me up from the restaurant, she asked how I felt. "Good," I replied. She'd been right. I wasn't proud of going to work, of sticking it through. Nor did I feel any sense of relief. But my spirits had been lifted. I couldn't grasp the psychology behind what she said. Even today, the feeling escapes me. And I'm not interested in the science either. I'd rather remain ignorant and accept her counsel. Because twenty-something years later, I'm still at the café, and her advice continues to ring true.

# Governor

A blacked out sedan reversed into the driveway, the type I'd only seen in action movies but never in real life. A besuited man stepped out of the passenger seat, positioned himself by the trunk, and assisted the driver in parking the car. They took their time nestling the car squarely between the lines. Then the man entered the café and went directly to the restroom in the back. "Ya viene el gobernador," the worker beside me said. I'd just started working again at the café as an adult. I had no idea what was going on.

The man exited the restroom and confirmed that the governor would be dining with us that afternoon. The First Lady of Texas arrived and grabbed a booth, where a couple of friends soon joined her. Then, an SUV pulled into the lot. The windows were so blacked out that if you pressed your forehead against one and blocked the sun's glare with your palms, you probably still couldn't see through the tint. I never had the cojones to try. The governor entered the restaurant with two other men and greeted everyone working there.

That was the first time I shook the governor's hand.

He had been a patron for many years. Mom and Papá shared

their stories with me. Papá had had rapport with him since he'd been Lieutenant Governor, which was before Bush took the Oval Office. When we were kids, whenever the Lieutenant Governor came into the café, Papà told us, and I always had to ask what a Lieutenant Governor was.

A couple of times, the governor hired us to cater his Christmas party. Catering wasn't a service we usually offered, but Mom made an exception for him. That night, Mom took the morning crew to the governor's mansion and provisioned his holiday bash. My favorite detail of Mom's story is that the governor ducked out of his own social event and hid in the back stairwell where he could savor his chicken chalupa in peace.

Blacked out cars kept backing in. The governor's left hand secured my forearm as we shook hands.

The governor and his wife rarely, if ever, dined alone. Friends and family almost always joined them, sometimes pushing a table to a booth or another table to make room for more guests. Their party rarely exceeded eight people, ten people max, not counting the four men with earpieces who always sat across the room. I rarely saw them eat, but they always asked us to refill the crushed ice in their unsweetened tea.

We never took reservations for customers, not even for the chief of state. Someone always came in early and put it together. They ordered guacamole and queso and margaritas before everyone else showed up. When it was time to order, the governor knew the procedure and queued up like everyone else. When the other customers saw the governor in the room, they shaped up. Hyde Park was a politically liberal neighborhood, but the governor of Texas was not. That didn't seem to be a problem. He went table to table and mingled as if on campaign and continued campaigning while he waited in line to order. Rarely did I see a disagreeable face.

Blacked-out cars kept backing in. This time, as the governor shook my hand, his left hand went past my forearm and cupped my tricep.

Cupping and securing the tricep, this style of handshake transported me to my days as a high school wrestler. It's the setup for one of my favorite takedowns: the fireman's carry. You start in a normal clinch position with your hand cupping the tricep, just as mine was cupped during our handshake. Then, you hook your right hand around the back of your opponent's neck, with your right forearm pressing against their chest, and you move back and forth, shucking until you see that their balance is off and their right leg is in front of their left. Then you make your move: shoot in, knee down, wrap the right thigh, and toss their cupped arm over your shoulder, like a fireman carrying somebody from a burning building. And the fun part: with the tricep and leg secure, you just roll back and down y'all go. If done correctly, you land in a favorable position.

For an instant, I thought, what if ... but the restaurant was too cluttered with tables and chairs for a takedown, and the floor wasn't matted. Anyway, the governor seemed like an easygoing guy who probably wouldn't mind too much if we had a quick roll. The four men in suits would probably mind, though. I once heard a rumor that they had boxing sessions and that one guy accidentally killed another guy while sparring. That's how hard the other guy was punched.

One day, I was tossing the trash, and on the way back from the dumpster, I noticed that one of those SUVs had a black bumper sticker with white letters that read: God bless our troops, especially our snipers. After that, I kept my wrestling whims to myself and made sure they had enough ice for their tea.

Blacked out cars kept backing in. When we shook hands, now the governor's left hand went past my forearm, past the tricep, and landed on the back of my shoulder.

There was a wall beside the register. One photo was a signed photo of Kirk Watson, the former and newly elected mayor, and former Texas state senator. We had a couple of famous UT football personalities: coach Brown and quarterback Colt McCoy. We'd recently added a signed photo of Lyle Lovett with Mom and Aunt Bobbie.

It was a humble wall, not one of these grandiose walls that

circumnavigate a restaurant dining room. I wondered how walls like that come to be. Do restaurant owners ask famous people for signed photos? Maybe famous people drive around with a cache of pre-signed frames in their trunks. "Hey, nice place! Can I put up a photo? I'll sign it."

One of our first photos was addressed to Papá, while he was still running the café. It was from the governor, and it was hung at eye level, where people could see it. A few customers said something about the governor to draw me into a political discussion, but I rarely took the bait. I tried my best to remain neutral about politics, especially while at work.

Blacked-out cars kept backing in. This time, the governor didn't shake my hand but came in for a hug, which caught me off guard. We chatted for a moment, and he asked how Papà was doing. Then he said something about fishing and Port Aransas and mentioned some other details only the family knew. His memory was impressive, and again, that caught me by surprise. It had been many years since the two of them talked, yet he could retrieve details about Papá.

After the governor's term ended, I saw him a couple more times at most.

I've never had a deep interest in politics, and I hope I never do. But I know where I'll start if I ever become interested in running for office. All you have to do is remember the name of everyone you've ever met and where they like to go on vacation.

# Green Chalupa

've noticed that Austinites love to boast about how Austin they
are. If they came to Austin for school, they wouldn't hesitate to
tell you—especially if that school was the University of Texas. Or
if they migrated to Austin for their first adult job and never left.
And who could blame anyone for not leaving? There's something
for everyone in Austin: the crystalline springs, the majestic live oak
canopies, the wailing guitars, the hippies on congas. But do people
from other cities brag the same way? I ask because I really don't
know. I've never lived anywhere else.

Some of our patrons love to remind me that they've been customers since West Lynn, the original location of the café. "I've been
coming in since before you were born," they say with swagger. While
most of these Austiny comments can be pesky, this one is not. It's
an honor to hear it. Assuming they were telling the truth, that person would have been a patron of the business for four decades. Few
accolades compare to retaining a patron for so long.

No matter how much I scour my memory, I can't picture the café
at West Lynn. I remember where it was, the businesses around it,

and the narrow walkway between the café and the corner store. Mostly, I remember the arcade games across the street in the run-down washateria: Space Invaders and Pac-Man. I can't picture the inside of the café, how the tables and chairs were laid out, or the wavy countertop that slithered around the dining area. But these veteran patrons remember it. It's proof of their Austinness.

After the café moved to Duval, my memories remain intact. The black and white checkered pattern of vinyl tiles on the dining room floor made the location approachable. Caribbean and Latino poster art hung from the walls. An old Brazilian Carnival poster popped out more than the others. And a marimba that looked like it had been struck too many times, or maybe not enough, was suspended from the back wall. Papá found it, who knows where, and decided that those beat-up ribs suited the café perfectly.

We hardly ever went to the café during peak hours, or anytime but weekdays shortly after school let out. The lull between lunch and dinner was the time to visit. We kids could sit wherever we wanted in the dining area without bugging anyone. Mom and Aunt Bobbie visited, too, and if Papá was there, we'd say hello.

Feeding me was both a cinch and impossible. I ate anything and everything. A tía from Venezuela once said she could clothe me, no problem, but if she had to feed me, I'd bankrupt her. At the café, I was most often fed bean and cheese nachos. At the time, they were larger and individualized. It wasn't until many years later that they converted to mound-style.

My sister and brother, Marisa and Luis, were also both a cinch and impossible to feed, but for opposite reasons. Unlike me, they were not voracious but selective about what they ate, so selective that Mom was forced into creative mode and hatched a hybrid dish for them. Mom's invention was so successful that for the next decade, Marisa and Luis refused to eat any other dish at the café. It came to be known as the Green Chalupa.

If an enchilada plate and a chicken chalupa had a child, it would be a green chalupa. The dish was straightforward: a chalupa shell topped with rice, then charro beans, in that order. The beans had to be drained before they were layered over the rice, so the chalupa shell didn't get too soggy. Then she'd add pulled rotisserie chicken, Monterey Jack cheese, and most importantly, the part that made it green, a generous pour of tomatillo on top. Finally, she'd nuke the chalupa until the cheese melted.

In hindsight, Mom's creation doesn't make sense. The chalupa was designed to be eaten with your hands, so it should have been simple, manageable, and not too heavy. The green chalupa was the opposite. It was messy; it crumbled and required a fork.

Whenever we visited the café, Mom went into the kitchen and crafted green chalupas for Marisa and Luis. No one else knew how to make them, at least not how Marisa and Luis liked them. I rarely asked for a chalupa, not because I didn't want them. I did. But I was strategic when it came to food. Marisa and Luis ate like sparrows and rarely cleaned their plates. All I had to do was wait. Once they were full, I'd swoop in and grackle up the remaining bits.

I recently asked Mom where she found the inspiration for the green chalupa.

"I saw Aunt Norris eating it one day when she was still working at the café."

"Oh. I always thought you invented it. Did you ask her how to make it?"

"No, I just looked at what it was and made it."

The truth didn't surprise me. Aunt Norris oozed creativity and was one of the better cooks in the family. But what difference does it make where the dish came from? Few ideas come from thin air, and fewer foods produce happy children and warm memories, not like the Green Chalupa.

# Something to Show

om and Papá made it clear we were expected to go to college. They drilled the importance of education into us, but not zealously. All three of us got through high school without a problem, although none of us graduated at the top of the class.

My younger sister, Marisa, earned a degree in civil engineering and, sometime later, added a stamp and those fancy letters after her name. Luis, the youngest, and I got a degree in business administration. However, Luis was displeased with his degree. He went back to school and back again, eventually earning a degree as a nurse practitioner with fancy letters after his name. Our society loves those letters. We put them on our LinkedIn, our business cards, and the plaque in our office. We love those letters because they are something to show.

An undergraduate degree didn't grant me those fancy letters. If I wanted to catch up to my siblings, I'd have to mortgage my life and get a master's. More education? Not worth it, I told myself. Who cares about letters and titles? Those are for people who need something to show. I've been told that I have a chip on my shoulder. For the longest time, I had no idea what that meant. This is what it means.

When Marisa or Luis came by the café, Mom joined their table. They would get margs and sip and chat and be merry without a worry in the world. I'd hold down the fort and cover for Mom. One of the cocineras always looked over at them while I was on the floor or at the register. She came up to me. "Moms sits with them and has a drink. She doesn't sit with you," Antonia whispered in my ear. "Ya ves. They go out to restaurants. Moms invites them to eat because they went to school and studied. Moms doesn't invite you because you didn't study. ¡Por burro!" We both laughed. She knew I studied at the university, too, but poked the bear anyway. Talking smack was how Antonia and I passed the time. "Ya. Por burro, ponte a trabajar."

Por burro - because you're an idiot, literally a donkey. The first time she said it, I chuckled. The second time, it stung a little. I thought saying it once was enough. If I let her see that she'd gotten to me, I'd never hear the end of it. As the saying goes, El que se lleva se aguanta. Don't horse around if you can't be bucked.

Forget the title and the acronym. I've heard it before. Immigrants say there is no greater shame than when you send your child to school, and they don't use their degree to make a career. They don't ejercer una carrera -pursue a profession, the one you studied for. These parents left their language, culture, country, and family to lift you overhead and nearly drowned as they waded across El Rio Bravo. They put their balls on the block and worked two jobs for decades so you could have the opportunity to study. And you didn't use your degree? It would be disingenuous to portray myself in that position. And by the same token, I thought it was unfair for others to apply that lens to me.

I have something to show for my studies, though not in the traditional sense. Certainly, a restaurant that has run for decades is something, and we have solid online reviews. Mom and I don't read them, though some people do, right? What about the ultimate metric of success: satisfied customers leaving with a smile? I wouldn't know how to prove it, maybe a scrapbook with laminated pages and pages of smiling customers.

My tasks at the café would have to be spruced up for my CV. Instead of cashier, I'd call myself a "sales associate." When I check on a table, I'd call that "customer experience." Let's say the customer strikes up a conversation, which goes well and bounces to another topic, then another. Soon we're bantering and bullshitting. That's "public relations." When I deal with complaints, that's "customer satisfaction." If Mom and I go out to dinner on a Sunday evening and bump into regulars who'd say hello, the simple courtesy of saying hello back could be the work of a "brand ambassador."

The list could go on to a second sheet, which would be a big no-no. I read somewhere that hiring managers only spend about fifteen seconds per résumé. The second sheet would never be seen. I need it, though, to show off the things I've learned. My college credentials wouldn't sum it up. I developed my skills on the job. You could call it a restaurant education, although I think it should be in Spanish, una educación de restaurante.

I ponder the word "educación" all the time. What it wasn't: saying mande usted so damn much when I was younger. As a kid, if I was at Mamá Abuela's and one of my tías called my name from the other side of the house, I'd yell back, "¡Qué!" ¡Agárrate! It didn't take colorful language or cuss words to get their blood pumping. All I had to say was ¡qué! and they'd go off. When I asked why, they'd reply educación.

In Spanish, educación means more than education. It's about good manners and treating others with respect, the way you were brought up to do. I get that. However, now older, mande isn't integral to the lesson they taught. Mande usted - at your service, at your command. I have a hard time buying into the submissiveness of that phrase.

The restaurant environment partly shaped my educación. Educación was about treading lightly on the emotions of customers and coworkers. It meant being gentle with people yet firm with business objectives. By no means was I perfect. Sometimes, I was a pushover, and I can be moody more often than I'd like to admit. I slipped up regularly, but I kept trying.

Where on my plaque or CV or business card do I put those snazzy letters that prove I received an educación from the restaurant? I still have faith that one day I'll open my mailbox, and by the grace of a greater divinity, I'll find a crisp manila envelope with my Certificado de Educación inside—something for that lonely gap on my wall.

# Unapplied

I don't know what this says about me, but I'm a sucker for up-and-coming ideas, especially when it comes to business. I can't help it. The new and shiny pulls me in. When I was a kid, Papá read the newspaper with his coffee every morning without fail. My version of reading the morning paper was not as well-rounded. I didn't care about local news or state or national politics. Give me new ideas, the new economy, give me the future.

There was one problem, however. Most of the new business ideas I read about were tech-related, and I was not a technical person, not in the slightest. I wasn't completely helpless. I knew how to attach files to an email and how to order an Uber. The bleeding edge, though, who has time to keep up? Machine learning, AI, blockchain, tokenization, AR, VR, the list goes on. And what does any of this mean? Is this tech really business-related, or is this tech for the sake of tech, fashion for the ambitious?

Knocking on tech isn't something I do with total ignorance. While living in Austin, the next Silicon Valley, learning about technology resonated with me. A few years ago, I enrolled in several online coding classes, attempting to acquire a new skill set. I picked up Python as my first computer language. For loops, while loops, integers, and strings. I learned the basics and then some. At the peak of my prowess, I could write scripts that scraped websites, which felt pretty good.

However, even after I reached that level, coding didn't do it for me. I wasn't tickled by it. Bona fide computer programmers lost themselves in their pet projects. While they were coding, time vanished. Dusk turned to dawn as they hacked away. But for me, five minutes felt like fifteen; two hours felt like four.

While learning to code, I heard this popular phrase: "Software will eat the world." That's where the techies got it wrong. What they were really describing was business, not software. The business world has no shame in its gluttony. Business has eaten the tangible world and the digital world, too. Next, philosophy was adapted and business-ized. Stoicism from Greek and Roman antiquity gained traction and was in vogue. Soft skills began to buzz and creep into my feed. Business has no limit. It's the customer who bankrupts the buffet. And there is no idea that better describes the insatiable appetite of business than one that just came into my feed: Kaizen.

Summarized, Kaizen is the idea of improving every day by just one percent. Half the reason Kaizen caught my attention was because it was Japanese. I have a soft spot for the Japanese and their culture, the cleavage between ancient traditions and futuristic methodologies, and the quirks nested in between. Like stoicism, Kaizen comes off as a modernized idea from the past, but it isn't. Kaizen sprouted from modern manufacturing. Finally, I thought, something attainable. Unlike coding, Kaizen was actionable, an idea I could finally apply to the café.

It was afternoon, time for my shift to start. Mom was at the register. When I asked how her shift had gone, she said, "I don't think we even got to four hundred today," which told me it had been excruciatingly slow. Four hundred was a fraction of a normal day, though typical of our lunches during the pandemic.

"I'm going to eat something real quick before going to Sam's," she said. Sam wasn't a special someone in Mom's life. Sam's was the big box store where she bought restaurant supplies, mostly non-food items like aluminum foil, paper towels, Styrofoam carry-out boxes, and plastic film.

In this age of digital shopping, going to a store seemed archaic. Grocery stores now offer curbside services; some even have delivery platforms that do the mundane for you. The future was happening. It was now. I thought of Kaizen, my one percent improvement for the day. I could automate Mom's task of going to Sam's, so she'd have more free time. I thought of the tap dance class she sometimes reminisced about, the classes she took as a girl. Maybe with this new free time, she'd re-enroll in classes. I practically patted my own back, I was so proud of myself.

Mom was in the corner booth, the most private spot in the dining area. I previously mentioned the idea of someone else shopping for her, but action was never taken. This time was different. Determined, I went to the Sam's website and got the ball rolling. They had their own in-house shopping service and an app to order from. This was going to be even easier than I'd thought. I sat across from Mom as she ate and downloaded the app.

"So, I just downloaded the Sam's app," I said. "What's on your list? Paper towels, for sure. We just ran out." I typed paper towels into the search bar. Several types came up. I scrolled down, found the ones we use, and added a box to the cart. "These are the ones we use, right?" I asked, turning the screen toward her like an eager child showing off.

"Yeah."

"What else is on the list?"

She mentioned more items, and I appended them to the app's shopping cart.

"Every time I go to Sam's, I see workers shopping for people. Are you going to place the order, and I'll pick it up?"

"Not yet. We still need to create an account and put in our

payment information. Also, it may be one of those things that we have to schedule in advance."

"Újule," she said.

"Or maybe we can. Let me see your phone. We'll download the app and put in all the information."

"I think you'll need my Google to get it," she said as she handed over her phone.

"I don't think so. It should be in the App Store. We probably don't need Google for this." I found the app and clicked to download. Apple ID requested permission to download.

"Hey, can you type in your Apple ID password so we can download this?"

"See! I told you."

"Not a big deal. Just put in your password, and it should be fine." Mom put the phone down, reached for her purse, and thumbed through loose papers until she finally found what she was looking for. She typed in her password, and the app began to download.

"And you know what? Since you're a preferred member of Sam's, they might even cut you a break, give you a discount on delivery.

"But I like going to the store." Mom blurted out. I looked over at her, head cocked, eyes squinted in confusion. "Going to Sam's is how I move my body. I walk around in there and lift heavy boxes into my cart. Going to Sam's is my exercise."

"Well, you can unload the car yourself when everything is delivered," I responded. I regretted hearing my unprocessed thoughts enter my ears. Thankfully, she didn't internalize my rude remark.

"Maybe I can get Luis to help me with it later," she said.

"Good idea. We don't have to do this now. When are you going next?"

"Probably on Saturday."

"Great, we'll schedule something then."

Mom's exercise comment ricocheted in my head. She was in her sixties and not one to exercise intentionally, so it was a blessing that she had a physical job. Restocking the fridge meant she had to lift cases of bottled beer and canned soda. She stood for hours, bussed tables, wiped counters, and swept the floor. For her age, Mom was in exceptional shape. Perhaps going to Sam's and lifting heavy boxes into her cart was part of the equation that kept her nimble. Saving extra time for tap dance, whose dream was that, really? Surely, there was something else to improve, another way to apply Kaizen to the business. Automating my mom's exercise plan seemed wrong.

I haven't opened the Sam's app since our talk. Like most apps on my phone, it goes unused and undeleted, a reminder of another unapplied idea.

On second thought, I sensed an inherent problem with Kaizen. It was like one of those challenges you see from an internet fitness guru, the push-up challenge: just one more push-up every day. Today, you can do fifty, tomorrow, one more. Every day, just one more. Massive strides were made in the first few weeks. Then, the results plateau until finally no strides are made at all. But the results from the beginning were so intoxicating. You can't get that one percent hogwash out of your skull. You go mad, an unquenchable neurosis.

# Stacy Paints a Sign

For as long as I can remember, the café has been counter service. The procedure couldn't be more straightforward: place your order at the register, pay, take a number, place it on your table, and wait for your food. The first steps in this sequence always tripped people up. Nothing against new customers who plopped themselves down at a table. How would they know the restaurant was counter service? Mom had a solution. She decided to commission a local artist she adored to make a sign for the café.

Stacy had already exhibited many of his works at the restaurant, including stained glass crosses, which were displayed in the front windows. Their relationship was symbiotic: Mom got free decor for the café, and Stacy could showcase his skills and sell his art. He had also painted a mural of a town that resembled old Austin behind a building near the restaurant. Every day, when we tossed the garbage, there it was, just beyond the dumpster. It reminded me of Hyde Park and the way West Campus used to look before the rise of luxury student housing. If Stacy could paint a mural on the entire side of a building, surely, he could paint a sign for Mom.

The sign he made was a gigantic male hand with the index finger pointing down. "Please Order Here," it read. We suspended it directly over the cash register.

The sign didn't work the way we'd hoped it would. As simple as the problem and solution were, people don't read signs, myself included. Maybe you can help me out here because there aren't many solutions to an unread sign. The only one I can think of is putting up a second sign for the first.

Mom never told me she wanted another sign. Stacy informed me when we were alone in the dining area. "Your Mom wants me to make a sign that tells people to order before taking a table." He looked over his shoulder and confessed, in a lowered voice, "I was thinking, what if for the sign, we had you dress up as a mariachi, and the mariachi held an instrument that read 'Please order before taking a table?"

My head was lowered as I listened. I agreed to his idea in a yeah-yeah-whatever way, thinking he was just brainstorming out loud. Then I looked up at him. His eyes were as big as loquats. He was serious about making a mariachi sign of me.

"Groovy. Do you happen to have a mariachi hat or guitar?"

"No, but I can probably get one."

"No problem. Do you have black pants?"

"I think so."

"Black though, they can't be navy or dark blue. They have to be black."

I just looked at him.

"No problem," he said. "I can pick some up from Goodwill. Actually, I think I have a pair that might fit you. We can use those."

I wasn't sure what painting style Stacy had in mind and wondered if he would doodle my face caricature style, a body with inflated beach muscles dressed in an all-black mariachi outfit. Not much time passed before I assumed his painting would be more life-like. He needed a realistic reference point from which to work; hence, he dressed me *en vivo* as a mariachi. It's hard to imagine a clearer indicator of seriousness than someone insisting your pants be black-black and not blue-black.

A few days later, we met at his place for the photo shoot. He lived a block away from the café, behind someone's house in one of those garage apartments. The pants he had were held together with safety pins, and the coat was as black as the pants. I put them both on. I thought nothing of his insistence on all black and wore brown bare-foot-style shoes with a toe box so wide they looked like ducks' bills —far from mariachi botines. Not that any of that would matter in the photo shoot. Surely, the sign would only be of my upper body. At worst, Stacy could paint my shoes black on the sign.

We went outside to take the photo in front of the building. The mariachi hat he had was too small and rested on the crown of my head. The final touch: he tied a pañuelo around my neck.

Then he handed me a cutout of an accordion. "Here. Hold this like you're playing a tune." I took it, looked down at the painted buttons and keys, and splayed my fingers over what I thought looked like a chord. My clammy hands transferred nervous moisture to the cardboard instrument.

"How does this look?"

"Groovy."

As he snapped the photos, doubt crept in. Why had I agreed to do this? This wasn't who I was. I had no idea how to play the accordion. What if someone who knew how to play the accordion called me out on the fake chord? One domino tumbled the next. I'm nei-ther Mexican nor a mariachi. The hat didn't fit, the clothes weren't mine. None of this was me. Appropriation wasn't in my wheelhouse then, but looking back now, that's what it was. I have friends from Jalisco, Tapatíos, the land of mariachi. What gave me the right to dress and act like this when I wasn't one of them? Hell, my friends didn't even act or dress like this. And there I was, posing for a sign that would be displayed at my workplace for the entire world to see. I should have just said no.

Less than two minutes and nearly a dozen photos later, we were done.

I bumped into Stacy several times but didn't ask him how the sign was coming along. Secretly, I hoped he'd forget about it, or (fingers crossed) the place developing the film would lose it.

More weeks went by. I didn't have to ask Stacy how the sign was coming along because he told me. He'd started on the head and face, the most challenging part according to him, and liked how it turned out. He even joked that he had a cutout in his living room, completely blank except for my face. Whenever he looked at the cutout, I looked back. In the morning, when he drank his coffee, I watched. Later in the afternoon, when he listened to classical music, my eyes were locked on him, my unflinching face always staring back.

Later, he told me he was working on another section of the sign. And then another. It seemed that every time we spoke, he was working on a new section. He wasn't the stereotypical wishy-washy artist I was hoping for. This was really going to happen. I should have known. Every time we sold one of his stained-glass crosses at the café, he diligently replenished it with another. I regretted having been so passive when we discussed the mariachi sign. I thought we were just bouncing ideas around out loud.

As much as I adored Mexican culture, la cocina y los dichos, I struggled to claim my Mexicaness. I've often asked Mom and my tías if Mamá Abuela was from Mexico City, and they always confirmed she was. I could even legally claim Mexican citizenship, but that wasn't enough.

Papá was from Venezuela, which made the water murkier. I was genetically closer to Venezuelans. However, when measuring my Mexicaness to my Venezuelaness, the former towered over the latter, if only because of proximity. I ate more Mexican food, and my Spanish was more Mexican than Venezuelan. I don't say pitillo, I say popote; I don't say chamo, I say chavo; I don't say patilla, I say sandía. But unlike my friends and coworkers, I wasn't from Mexico. I was born and raised in Texas.

The day came unexpectedly. I was wiping the tables, sweeping the floor, or thumbing along on my phone when a life-sized object wrapped in black butcher paper appeared on the patio. We had no idea what it was until I remembered the sign Mom commissioned. Stacy was nowhere to be found.

I hesitated to unwrap it, but when I did, it was me, sure enough. The sign was my exact height. My hands were the same size as in real life, frozen in time, performing the same fake accordion chord.

The longer the sign stood there, the more I felt I could own it. Colors, proportions – everything was true to my memory of the photo shoot, almost to a fault. The shoes were exactly as I'd worn them – brown and unfashionably wide. Would it have been that hard to paint them black to match the rest of the suit instead of immortalizing my lack of style?

But as time passed, I was glad Stacy hadn't decided to paint my shoes black. It's not that I saw my brown shoes as wabi-sabi, the beauty found in imperfection. Instead, I considered the eyesore as my poser defense, which begs the question, is a poser still a poser if he admits to posing? No mariachi worth his weight in Tajín could get away with wearing brown shoes with a black suit. He'd be booted out of the band. Call me a poser. I can own that, and I can own the shoes on the sign.

# Duo

For the second year in a row, I convinced Mom to close for a week during the summer, arguably our slowest season. After a bountiful spring, there was no use in grinding our bones over summer scraps. Closing for a week was the only way we could both get off at the same time, the only way I could justify getting on an airplane without feeling I was leaving Mom to fend for herself.

It took years of pressure, but she finally caved in. "It's not about the money," she said, trying to defend her position. "I like to stay open for our customers." We agreed on dates to close and reopen a month and a half in advance, giving the crew time to plan their own vacations.

When I asked Mom what she had planned, she mentioned Mexico City. A month went by. Summer vacation was a week away. When I asked again, her answer was San Antonio with Aunt Susie and Houston to visit Marisa. She had no plans to fly anywhere. On the other hand, I was itching to explore and knew exactly where I was going: Sayulita on the Pacific coast. I'd spend one week in Mexico: three days at the beach and three days in Guadalajara.

It had been years since I'd visited Guadalajara. A couple of my friends lived there, and I looked forward to reuniting with them. From Guadalajara, it was a five or so-hour drive to Sayulita, depending on las curvas, the curvy section of road that went down the mountain, one lane each way. Assuming no wrecks, broken-down trucks, fallen trees, or whatever magic Mexico could muster, five hours it was.

I wanted three things from my trip: to see my friends, get sand, saltwater, and sun on my skin, and buy a pair of doomsday huaraches. A few years back, I noticed a friend had a nice pair, and I couldn't get the design out of my head. I even took a photo to remember better. They were leather with truck-tire soles, durable, and heavy enough to dish out a chanclazo if I was ever in a pinch. I was so obsessed I was willing to spend an entire vacation day scouring the mercado for those huaraches.

Guadalajara is one of the largest cities in Mexico, and I was convinced that it had a monster mercado. Shallow research on Google sent me to San Juan de Dios, the largest indoor market in Latin America.

The building was the size of a city block with multiple floors. One of the middle floors was almost entirely filled with food vendors. The top floor was trendy American fashion, most of which seemed counterfeit. The bottom level had more traditional Mexican things: colorful bags, sweet confections, palo santo, and those brujería powder packets that cured poverty or a verbose spouse. Somewhere on the bottom level, I found the leather section where the huaraches were. There were dozens of styles in varying color combinations. I had the photo on my phone, wedged who knows where in the middle of hundreds of other useless photos. I told myself I'd know the huaraches when I saw them.

The mercado was teeming with persistent salespeople – "A sus órdenes," "¿Qué busca usted?" "Mándame" – all of them insisting that the huaraches they sold were what I was looking for. They met the criteria but didn't look like my memory of my friend's huaraches, which had an uncommon crisscross design.

After an hour, I was lost in the bowels of the mercado, nada. I thought the design must have been discontinued, and I'd have to settle for something else. And how would I find my way out? It wasn't unpleasant to be lost in the leather section with saddles and riding gear, belts, and jackets and boots. I got drunk on the aroma of leather.

Finally, I found the huaraches, although the crisscross pattern wasn't exactly how I remembered it. The lady in charge of the stall called me joven, although she didn't look much older than I was.

"Do you have these in size eight?" I'm size eleven in the States, and size forty-four in Europe. In huaraches, I'm a size eight. I cherished the difference, glad Mexico hadn't become totally Westernized yet.

"Yes, I have it. Give me one moment." She turned and called a name. A boy came out from behind one of the displays. "Can you get me these in size eight, please?" She looked back at me. "Go ahead and take a seat. I'll bring them to you."

I tried them on. They were the ones, but they were off-white with a hint of seafoam green, not brown like my friend's shoes.

"They feel great. How much?"

"Four hundred and fifty pesos."

"Can I pay with a card?"

"Claro." She called the boy again. I looked over and saw him in a nook behind the display, slouched over a small screen. "Can you charge him for these huaraches?" Without an inkling of urgency, he got up from his stool and pulled out the hand-held terminal. I stuck my card in, paid, and signed. No words were spoken. After the transaction, he returned to his nook, stool, and screen.

"Is he your son?" I asked the lady.

"He is."

"You know, I work with my mother, too, in a restaurant."

"Es muy bonito."

"Es bonito. Y difícil también," I said, sympathizing with her bored son.

Maybe my words landed wrong because she didn't respond, so I thanked her and left.

Idiot me. Why ruin a wholesome moment by telling her how difficult working with family could be? Working with Mom wasn't arduous, at least not now that I was older. When I was younger, I felt self-conscious about working with her. A decade and a half later, manning the restaurant with Mom was a breeze, a gift in disguise, an experience I will forever hold dear.

A couple of months later, I flew to Guadalajara for a long weekend and returned to the San Juan de Dios Mercado. This time, I felt a little guilty for leaving Mom and Aunt Bobbie on their own. The tire treads on my huaraches still had a solid 15,000 miles left, but I wanted to immerse myself in the cloud of leather smells again and to visit the mother-son duo. I purposefully wore the huaraches I'd purchased from her and looked forward to showing them off. This time, I wouldn't be so sloppy with my words.

I struggled to retrace my steps through the labyrinth of leather. Turns out, many vendors sold huaraches with that crisscross pattern. I kept seeing them, but I never found the mother-son duo. I never saw them again.

# Salamander Tacos

It wasn't until I was older that I realized having a parent from another country was an advantage. Sure, we kids missed out on plenty, mostly traditional American experiences. For instance, we weren't allowed to spend the night at a friend's house until we were much older. "That's what primos are for," Mom and Papá said. Stay with your cousins. Summer camp? Forget it. There were no marshmallows, pinecones, splash wars in the lake, or whatever kids did at camp. For me, camp was working at the restaurant with Papá.

Aside from that, having a foreign-born father wasn't bad. In high school, many of my friends admitted they never understood much of what Papá said. Even after four decades in the States, he had a thick accent. My brother Luis and I made a pastime of imitating him. We'd call Mom E-Te-La instead of Estella. Or say "cut it" instead of "cut it out." Luis was exceptionally talented at impersonating Papá.

While parroting him amused us, we struggled with much of his humor. When I was finally old enough to go to Barton Springs on my own, Papá asked what I'd been up to. I told him I went swimming at the springs. He replied that the next time I went to the springs,

I should bring back some salamandras so we could put them on the grill and make salamandra tacos. He was kidding, but I didn't think much of his joke. If anything, his comment seemed ridiculous and bizarre. The Barton Springs salamander was an endangered species. I dismissed the comment as only comical to someone from a different culture.

After years of learning what Mexican food was and all the different styles of tacos, the notion of a salamander taco seems wittier than it did the first time I heard it. Mom told me that when she was a young girl, she'd dart home to eat something between school and dance lessons. She was always so ravenous that she'd eat anything. Mamá Abuela usually whipped up a taco for her. One day, the taco was so delicious she asked for another, but Mamá Abuela replied, "Sorry, that was the last one." Mom asked what it was. Mamá Abuela replied, "Armadillo."

One summer, I had the privilege of staying in Guanajuato for two months. During my stay, I often went to el Jardín de la Unión. Everyone went to el centro in the evening–twitterpated teens, energetic kids, abuelos on every bench– the entire pueblo was there. I'd always pass a particular street stall where meat sizzled and bubbled on the plancha. The smell was so pungent I could smell it through my eyes and held my breath for half a block. After weeks of holding my breath, I finally asked the señora I was staying with what was cooking in that stall. She told me they sold tripas, animal intestines.

After that, whenever I saw the word tripas written on the side of a trailer or menu, I turned the other way. I always ordered something else, anything else, never tripas. Nearly a decade passed before I finally reconsidered my position. My friend Agustín and I went out for tacos, and he asked if I'd ever had tripas. I said no. He said they were one of his favorites and ordered four tripas tacos. I decided to take a chance and requested two tripas and two of something else, in case they were awful.

The tripas tacos were incredible.

I went back repeatedly, ecstatic over the new flavor. I couldn't get enough. I boasted about my experience to Rogelio, our planchero, and asked him what he thought. He also adored them and told me to order them doraditas, fried golden brown, the next time. He recommended a yellow trailer off St. Johns and gave me the name of someone to ask for.

More travels and trailers later, especially over the border, I realized there was more to Mexican gastronomy than what I found at the supermarket. A taco made with meat from a cow could be many things: bistec, suadero, tripas, cabeza, carnaza, picadillo, lengua. Barbacoa was beef some of the time, though in Mexico, it could also be chiva, goat. Beyond the frontier, deeper into Mexico, there were ojo, labio, ubre, sesos – eye, lips, udder, brains. I struggle to recall the last time I purchased cow lips from the grocery store. And how would the butcher at H.E.B. look at me if I asked him how their udders were looking today? North of the border, in the land of everything, we don't have to use the odd cuts. We don't have to hunt or forage. We don't have to be so resourceful.

In another country, back in the day, or perhaps today in a pueblo down by a creek, the salamander taco might have been nothing to laugh at. It might have been the pueblo's specialty. Maybe salamander tacos were once a delicacy, but the pueblo ate every last salamander, which wouldn't be funny at all, although it would make what Papá said that day comical if that type of humor is your thing.

# I Thought She Thought

The stories I assumed to be true as a kid but discovered untrue as an adult. A plethora of false truths disappeared as I got older, but not all of them went away. Some lingered well into adulthood, such as the real reason Mom went back to work.

For the longest time, I assumed Mom returned to work out of boredom. We lived in a traditional family setting. Papá went to work while Mom stayed home with us kids. And from what I saw, that was shorthand for scrubbing every visible surface of the kitchen, mopping, vacuuming, and cooking. Mom washed every article of our clothing, every bedspread and towel. She picked us up from school, helped with our homework, and hauled us to friends' houses and after-school activities. She still remembers the names of childhood friends I haven't seen in decades.

The scope of Mom's tasks as el ama de casa went well beyond domestic duties. She was always emotionally present, our personal entertainer. She took us back in time, telling us stories about when she was a little girl or stories that happened when we were too young to remember. My favorite story was about how she learned to drive a stick shift car when she was only twelve. She started in her drive-way, backing up and pulling in, shift drive, shift reverse, shift drive, shift reverse, then graduated to the road. As a girl, she bought cig-arettes for the madam who lived next door, driving the woman's car without a license, and buying smokes when she was underage. When she told this story at a recent Christmas gathering, a new de-tail emerged. While buying the madam's cigarettes, Mom managed to sneak in a joy ride with her best friend Trina.

We reaped immeasurable benefits from Mom staying home. But at what cost? I can hardly fathom the boredom of being an ama de casa, interacting only with children and facing the abyss of house chores. How is that sustainable?

Then, Mom had a realization. After over a decade of house arrest, she thought, "¡Ya! Enough!" She needed to get out of the house, a change of scenery, a job.

Her last employer was no longer an option, and few jobs were available. She needed part-time work that would allow her to main-tain her priorities as el ama de casa but also get her out of the house. I was never told how arduous her escape efforts had been, but even-tually, she found work that met her criteria.

Her career at the café began.

That's the story I conveniently imagined for over twenty years, nearly the entire duration of Mom's café career. One day, when we were swapping stories, I revisited her flight from the mundane.

"You went to work because you were bored, right?"

"I went to work because I wanted a new car."

I knew my favorite Mom stories inside out. Zina, the Russian madam, was a former ballet dancer who had managed to escape the Soviet Union. Mom said the madam called her "darling," imi-tating the madam's voice.

Mom's life happened right under my nose, but I had no idea how her story unfolded. I only knew how I forced the pieces into place for my understanding.

Mom wanting a new car made sense. What would hauling three

children around town for over a decade do to a 1984 Honda Accord? She took us to school, to Mamá Abuela's, to and from friends' houses, to thrift stores and garage sales, followed by car sickness, followed by 7up, followed by burgers at Nau's drug store–Mom's poor Honda. We punctured the speakers behind the backseat with our little fingers, so the sound quality was gone forever. Not that it mattered. The AC didn't work, so for half the year, we toured the city with the windows down, wind full blast. The tape player was out of commission, too. A dirt dauber wasp once thought the cassette port would make a lovely home and began to build a nest she never finished. We broke some things out of curiosity. Specifically, the plastic guides for the safety belts. "How far can this plastic thingy bend back?" *SNAP.* "Oh." And by "we," I mean "I."

Mom continued working at the café well after she got her new car, so it's fair to assume she enjoyed getting out of the house. And she did it without neglecting her post as ama de casa. The house was still clean, and our clothes were still washed. We never missed a meal. She still found the time to repeat the stories we liked and brought home new ones. Don't ask me how she did it. I can only imagine.

We never got rid of the tormented Honda. Years later, Mom taught me how to drive stick in that car. And I inherited it, my first set of wheels, complete with punctured speakers, snapped seat belt guides, a broken AC, and the caked mud the dirt dauber left in the tape deck.

# Feet and Knees

When I say restaurants are touchy-feely, I don't just mean that in the emotional sense. We love to touch and feel each other. Some people love hugging, others prefer spanking butts. Some like mock fighting, not really hitting, but playing. One of our plancheros, Rogelio, loved to hug. Monserrat, a cocinera, was much taller than he was, so when they hugged, he'd rest his head against her chest like a child seeking comfort. He was married, and so was she, but not to each other. They'd worked together for a decade and a half and gone to dances together in a purely platonic way. Mauricio saw them hugging and wanted to rest his head on the pillows, too. Montserrat laughed and hugged him back. Mauricio was a hugger and loved to connect in that way. He sometimes hugged me.

Hugs usually happened when the restaurant was slow. A good hug can't be hurried. It needs its own pace, which is why this particular hug seemed odd. It was Saturday brunch, one of the busier shifts of the week. I'd finished taking an order at the register and returned to the kitchen to submit the ticket when I saw Mauricio's arm around Aunt Bobbie. I thought he just wanted a hug and returned to the register. As I was walking back to the front of the restaurant, I glanced at Sara, one of the cocineras, and made my eyes big. She did, too, as if we were saying, "Did you see them hugging?" I took another order and returned to the kitchen with the ticket. Now Andres, the other prep cook, was close to Aunt Bobbie. He and Mauricio weren't hugging Aunt Bobbie, they were stabilizing her.

I rushed over. "What's going on?"

"Es que–"

"I can't feel my leg," Aunt Bobbie said.

I thought, please God, not another stroke. Andres guided Aunt Bobbie to the back office and pulled out a chair for her.

I hurried to the front, grabbed my phone and pulled up Tía Lola's number, then rushed back to Aunt Bobbie."Do you want me to call Tía Lola?"

"No. It's just my leg. It's numb."

"I can call someone if you like." I hit Tía Lola's contact.

"No, papi. I'm fine. My leg is just numb."

"Are you sure?" I canceled the call.

"Really, I'm fine. It's my right leg, not even on my stroke side."

She insisted that she was okay, probably because she didn't want to be a burden. I honored her word and reluctantly went back to the register, then bussed a couple of tables and returned to the office. She was sipping iced tea through a straw. "How are you feeling?"

"I'm feeling better. I can feel my leg again." She took another sip. "This has happened before. I've learned to just relax when it happens." She grinned and released a deep breath, her shoulders lowered as she exhaled.

"Okay. Just let me know if you need something ... a ride home, whatever."

"I'm fine, thank you."

I took more orders, bussed more tables. After twenty minutes, I returned to see how Aunt Bobbie was. She had pulled her chair to the counter with the forks, knives, and napkins in front of her.

The rush had slowed down, so I visited with her while she rolled silverware. She said something about writing a will. A friend had told her that it would be valid even if written on a napkin, so long as it was signed – and maybe notarized. I thought a notarized napkin would be better than nothing. Aunt Bobbie later admitted that she wasn't ready to go. She said she still had to cross-stitch a few Christmas stockings. She'd made one for me nearly forty years earlier and one for almost every family member, which was no small feat considering the size of our family.

Aunt Bobbie was out of commission, but she was rolling silverware. A Zapata quote came to mind, the type of quote you'd see on a fridge magnet: "I prefer to die on my feet than live on my knees."

Back in the day, Aunt Bobbie had been a force of nature. You could put her anywhere—upfront with customers, the grill, the dishes. She was a beast wherever she was. Hell, you could put her in the dish pit and at the register at the same time, and somehow, she'd get it done. Decades later, she wasn't the pistol she used to be. Mom tried to relieve her of the heavy burdens and assign them to others.

Aunt Bobbie had had two strokes. She had arthritis in her hands and a bum shoulder. The possibility of something happening to her was uncomfortably real. But sitting at home all day wasn't the right solution for her. She'd always lived on her feet. I thought work was part of what kept her going. Neither Mom nor I had the heart to tell her she couldn't work at the café anymore. Work was her connection to the world. Who were we to take that away?

The challenge was finding the right balance—work that wasn't too strenuous but preserved her dignity. La plancha was out of the question. Most of the plates were too heavy for her arthritic hands. She could take orders at the register, but Mom didn't want her up front during peak hours. She could wash dishes and roll silverware. She could clean. When we needed something from the store, she went, which was a huge help. And we still needed her to make her famous flan because she wouldn't share the recipe with anyone. She never wrote it down, not even on a napkin.

I still think about that Zapata quote. I misuse it and take it out of context. Death to a revolutionary, swift, on your feet, dead before you hit the ground. But to romanticize extraordinary words by applying them to my tía seemed wrong. Not because she wasn't extraordinary. She was. But because dying while doing the dishes is not the same as dying para el pueblo. Who am I to say? Aunt Bobbie was in the back office, sipping tea and rolling silverware with a numb leg and refusing to let me call anyone. Perhaps she thought otherwise.

# Chicken Suit

In bold blue letters, a sign outside the café read:
"HAPPY HOUR
MON - SAT, 2 - 6."
It was both vague and to the point, perhaps the only promotional offer we ever made. People sometimes asked what happy hour was, and I'd respond, "Three-dollar beers and five-dollar ritas."

"No food?"

"Just beers and ritas."

I remember Papá bragging, "I've never spent a dime on advertising. We've been word of mouth since West Lynn." Years later, I, too, was proud that we still didn't need to advertise.

But during my tenure at the café, advertising became much easier. Social media was in the mix, and businesses leveraged their power. I wasn't much of a media guy, but I created an account on one of the platforms just to see what the hype was about. It seemed like the hip thing to do.

My first post was a chicken chalupa with avocado. I placed the plate on a patio table in front of a blooming jasmine and snapped several angled photos. The green lettuce on the chalupa blended with the jasmine's darker green leaves and soft yellow flowers. I felt artsy and pleased that I could still claim the café had never spent a dollar on advertising.

I only published a few posts before I halted my experiment. Something didn't sit well. Turns out social media consumed a lot of time, more than I expected. Then, news broke that social media was just as addictive as cigarettes. Since I already drank and sometimes smoked, I couldn't afford more vices, so I axed social media.

In Austin, everything slows down during the summer. The manager of the gelato shop next door used to joke that summer was even too hot for gelato. His sales, like ours, were in the gutter.

One day, at the cusp of afternoon and evening, when the aroma of jasmine was a faint memory, no orders came in, and most of our prep was done. Some of the crew couldn't stand putzing around and found other things to do. Some just lolled around, and I let them. They always busted their tails when they had to. Plus, I wasn't that great at cracking a whip.

"I don't like it when it's this slow," the cocinera said.

"Me neither," I replied. "Don't worry. They'll be here soon."

She sighed. "Work feels so much longer when it's like this."

"I know."

"Julio, why don't you put on el disfraz de pollo and go outside and bring people in?"

"A chicken costume?" I laughed. "It's too hot to be outside in a chicken costume, nor do I have one."

"You need a chicken costume. That would bring people in, de volada."

"What makes you think that?"

"I know."

"I don't have a chicken costume."

"Well, you need one."

"Fine, I'll get one. But *you're* gonna be the one who wears it."

"No, *you* are."

"And why me?"

"Because it's your job to bring people in."

"And you?"

"I'm the cook. Who's going to cook if I have the chicken suit on?"

"I'll cook."

She laughed as if the idea of me cooking was funnier than me wearing a chicken suit.

"You wouldn't last one hour back here."

She was right.

Every so often, I mused over the chicken costume and whose job it was to wear it. I could only imagine wearing it for two consecutive days in the street. The suit would still be salty and damp from the day before.

Later, on a slow morning before the lunch rush, the lavatrastes got the same idea. "Hey, why don't you put on a chicken outfit and go to the street corner?" Again, with the chicken suit. The cocinera on the evening shift rarely saw the lavatrastes who worked mornings. Where was this idea coming from?

"You think that would work?"

"Claro," the lavatrastes said with a grin.

"Well, I don't have a chicken suit."

"Go buy one."

"I don't know where they sell chicken suits."

"¡El internet! You can find everything on the internet."

"Ok, I'll buy one. But *you're* going to wear it."

"Me? Look at me," he said, waving his hands up and down his torso. "I wouldn't fit in the costume. I'm fat and short, and you, tall and skinny. It would fit you perfectly. You would be good at it too, much better than me. Plus, who would wash the dishes if I were in the suit?"

"Don't worry. While you're outside in the suit, I'll wash the dishes."

"¡Ja!" He exaggerated. "You wouldn't last one shift washing dishes."

They must have gotten the idea from another restaurant, perhaps a Pollo Regio, known for the gigantic bird that danced in the streets, a special dance that made it rain dollars. I struggled to connect the dots. How would a person dressed as a chicken, doing a cumbia in the street, persuade people to buy chicken?

During the gap between Christmas and the New Year, we closed the café, and I used the time to explore Mexico. While walking from a friend's house to the local tianguis many blocks away, I heard Latino-style club music coming from a speaker. On the corner, a couple of people were doing a promotion. One spoke into a PA system while the other danced, dressed as a chicken.

The person in the chicken suit was animated and surprisingly in touch with her body. She did a simple one-two step with a complicated shoulder shimmy and, later, a more basic move, sliding her head side to side, so la cresta flopped.

I stopped momentarily to admire the dancing chicken, then kept walking. The music was too deafening to endure. Just past the booming PA and the dancing bird was a store that sold rotisserie chickens. The place was called El Pechugón, which literally means "the large-breasted one." They sold rotisserie chickens, potatoes, and maybe one other side dish. Two massive rotisseries roasted five times the number of chickens we could roast at the café. More impressively, the tiny storefront was slammed with a line about twenty people deep. This must be what the crew at the café had been harping about.

Over the years, the compound interest we yielded from our word-of-mouth campaign had been more than enough. We got on just fine without advertising or a clicky social media presence. But if the summer blues extended into the fall or started early in the spring, or if the busy season dwindled to a dispirited trickle, I didn't have to fret. I'd just buy a PA and a chicken suit, blast a catchy cumbia, and learn how to shimmy.

# I Am Your Grandson

I suspected our recipes were modified but had no way of proving it. Mamá Abuela contributed her recipes to the business, but over the years, they became a multigenerational game of telephone. We recited the message as best we could, hoping to accurately relay something that had been said decades before. I couldn't remember her cooking clearly enough to distinguish her dishes from those we were serving.

Proof came on a Saturday morning when Tía Lola ordered huevos rancheros for breakfast. Less than two minutes passed before she called me over to her table.

"This isn't how the rancheros are made," she said. I gave her plate a quick scan: beans, bacon, ranchera sauce, eggs, potatoes, aguacate, tortillas. Everything was there.

"Looks like you got everything on the plate," I assured her.

"No. The tortilla on the bottom doesn't have any chile on it." I looked over her plate again.

"The ranchera goes on top of the eggs."

"And on the tortilla. The tortilla should have chile on it, too."

We looked at each other, puzzled, both convinced we were right.

"Don't worry about it," she said.

"No, no. I can get ranchera on the tortilla, too."

"It's fine."

"Are you sure? It's an easy fix."

"No, really. It's okay."

I didn't push the issue further. If she said it was fine, it was fine. Plus, Saturday mornings were hectic. Aunt Bobbie had a line at the register. No need to repair an airplane mid-flight.

I've had our huevos rancheros many times. It was a top-selling breakfast plate for good reason. However, Tía Lola had a point. I've seen huevos rancheros in mercados and on Mexican cooking shows. Many times, the tortilla is dipped in chile before it's put on the comal. If Tía Lola remembered the huevos rancheros with this detail, there's a good chance that that step was phased out sometime in the past.

I'm guessing that years before I started working at the café, the cooks made the modification to streamline the process. Who could blame them? They had a plethora of meals to plate in just a few hours. When there was a battle between efficiency and the integrity of Mamá Abuela's recipes, efficiency sometimes won. Even if the tortilla started dry, sin chile, it didn't stay dry. The yolk was broken almost immediately, and the beans and ranchera seeped into the tortilla shortly thereafter.

Tía Lola would remember how Mamà Abuela prepared the dish better than I did. Any of my tías would. For sure, Mom remembered Mamá Abuela's cooking. Was she aware of the tortilla sin chile? My memory of Mamá Abuela's cooking is mostly void. I remember eating flautas with guacamole, and a particular enchilada with crema on top.

I haven't forgotten Mamá Abuela's remedy for bored children, also how I earned my first dollar: sweeping the porch. By then, I had forgotten Spanish and only spoke English. We went to the front porch, and she brushed the broom against the floor several times before handing it to me. I took fewer than half a dozen strokes before she snatched it back and said something in Spanish. Then she demonstrated again: firm wrists, not flimsy.

Mamá Abuela told us nietos that if we didn't eat our vegetables, our toes would look as funky as hers. Mom translated for us, though there was no need. Her toes were enough to get the message across.

When Mamá Abuela became ill, Mom visited her often at the South Austin Medical Center, sometimes dragging us with her. I don't remember much, except that we were bored, and there was no porch for us to sweep.

Mamá Abuela was released with a nasty incision on her chest, but there were complications, and she was soon hospitalized again.

Mom told us that people were always at their house when she was growing up. Nothing brought Mamá Abuela more pleasure than feeding guests. Nostalgic for absent memory, I'd ask about Mamá Abuela's cooking. Although I knew what Mom would say, I always found solace in her answer.

What was authentic about our cooking at the cafè, and what had been modified for economy? After forty years of telephone, how would I know the difference? A cook might begrudgingly add garlic to the salsa recipe, only to leave it out one day. Something about mal aliento, bad breath. Now, whose recipe is it? Who can tell the garlic was left out? Many times, I can't.

Decades before her recipes were showcased at the café, Mamá Abuela cooked for affluent Old West Austin clients. Did she make dishes for clients like she did for her family at home? Or did she prioritize economy over authenticity? If she were alive and came to the café for dinner, would she approve of our interpretation of her recipes?

Surely, authenticity and economy don't have to be dichotomous. And why should I care if some people missed the ranchera sauce on the bottom tortilla or peas and carrots in the rice? I say, 'I don't care,' and 'who cares,' that's how I simplify decisions and move forward. But no matter how many times I say it, deep down, I do.

Mamá Abuela, it's unfortunate our time together was so limited. At least, that's how it feels for me. My memories are faint. And please don't ask me about the recipes we say are yours. I'm not sure they really are, but I promise I've them written down somewhere. And though that's embarrassing to confess, I hope it's okay with you.

# A Cien

The lavatrastes punched his timecard. He was in an extra good mood, smiling almost to the point of laughter.

"Julio, ¿cómo andas?" he asked.

"Bien. ¿Y tu?"

"¿Andas a cien?" Are your batteries full?

"Simón. Ando a cien. Ya sabes." Yeah. They're full, you know it.

"A cien..." he chuckled. "Haciéndote güey nomás." They're full, full of shit.

Everyone within earshot erupted in laughter. He began by asking how I was feeling, then reversed into a schoolyard putdown. Such insults doubled as bonding and a backhanded Spanish lesson.

# Milpero

The phone rang. "Can you get that?" Mom called. She had a line of people at the register.

"I can't."

Mom picked up the phone, "Julio's, can you hold ... ?" She placed the phone on the counter before they could respond. "I have someone on the line. Can you get that?"

"I'm sorry. I can't," I shouted back. I wasn't trying to be a brat. Plates without legs got cold. Dirty tables have to be bussed before the grackles arrive. Food is pushed out of the kitchen and dishes crashed back to the sink area in a synchronized manner. Empty hands mean faster feet or falling behind.

While dropping off a bin of dirty dishes in the sink area, I noticed a reused sour cream tub with salsa verde in it. Unlike the verde we used for the enchiladas, this one was creamy. The health department didn't like us to wash and repurpose food containers, but sometimes we did it anyway. The lavatrastes managed to pull off a salsa verde before the shift roared and the blenders sloshed tequila with ice and orange liqueur. What she didn't use in the salsa was left in the colander by the clean dishes.

"Have you seen the tomatillos I used in la salsa?" she asked.

I was unloading dishes from the bus bin, hurrying to take food to the table before it became tepid.

"They're very beautiful tomatillos." She told me the type of tomatillos she used, but I didn't catch the name. We'd been working together for years, and I'd stopped keeping track of her concoctions, but in a fleeting gap between tasks, I grabbed a tortilla chip from one of the baskets and timidly dipped it into the reused container. The salsa was thick and stuck to the chip. Only after you're sure the salsa is good do those dips turn to hearty dunks and, eventually, greedy scoops. The salsa was agreeable. "Está muy buena," I told her. "What did you put in it?"

"Serranos, cilantro ... take a look in the colander. What I didn't use is still in there." She was beyond busy. I looked in the colander and noticed the tomatillos she was talking about. They were a bit smaller, but with a distinct purple hue, as if they'd been bruised. "These are the tomatillos you were talking about. What are they called again?"

"Son milperos, tomatillos milperos."

I couldn't believe what I heard, but Mexican Spanish, at least the bit I've learned, can be informal and inventive. For example, a tractor's backhoe is called mano de chango – monkey's hand. This inventiveness was utilized in our kitchen, too. The small saucepan we used for nearly everything was called el mil usos– the thousand-uses. "¿Dónde está el mil usos?" – "Where is the thousand-uses?" – "Where's the small saucepan?" So when the lavatrastes told me the tomatillos she used in the salsa were called milperos, what I heard was mil pedos, a thousand farts.

Kitchen humor is notorious for drifting south, which was fine with me. How can anyone expect a crew to show up to work on time, and bust their tails every day, without allowing some room for play? What if she wasn't joshing with me, and they were really called tomatillos mil pedos, thousand-farts tomatillos? Mexican gastronomy already had a reputation. Something about that beautiful purple hue, something about the smaller size. Maybe I should stick to shallow dips after all.

The lavatrastes had a sense of humor, but she rarely strayed in that direction. It was loud and busy, we had our masks on, certainly our communication was off. "They're tomatillos mil pedos?" I asked.

"Yes, milperos." This time, I heard her correctly.

"Milperos, from la milpa?" From the cornfield?

"Yes, what did you think I said?"

"I thought you said mil pedos."

She erupted in laughter.

"No. From la milpa." The cocineros laughed once they caught whiff of the joke, though not with the same gusto. There were too many tickets in the queue for that. Soft Rs and Ds have a way of sounding similar, especially at the end of a word.

That evening, the lavatrastes and I happened to eat together. The others were either too tired or just wanted to clean up and leave. She'd brought a dozen eggs from the chickens she kept at home. Dinner was simple: fried eggs, corn tortillas, and the salsa she'd made with those distinctive tomatillos.

I remembered that not long before, a cocinera and the other lavatrastes, both from Guatemala, were giggling and making references to la milpa. I wasn't curious at first. But they went on and on, and eventually, I had to ask what la milpa was. The lavatrastes replied, "La milpa is where they harvest corn." So much giggling over a boring cornfield? I assumed milpero could also be vernacular for homegrown, given the dishwasher's eggs and her do-it-yourself attitude. Tomatillos milperos - tomatillos grown in one's field or vegetable garden.

After a brief visit with the browser, I discovered that tomatillos milperos are known for their diminutive size, unique taste, and beautiful purple markings. A wormhole of hyperlinks later, I learned that a milpero was someone who worked in la milpa, a cornfield, and that the word milpa is derived from a cultivation technique used by the ancient Mesoamerican people to sustainably grow multiple crops on the same land at the same time. The trio of corn, beans, and squash was known by North American peoples as the Three Sisters.

I can't imagine sisters always working together so well, but these three are particularly synergetic. The first sister, corn, provides the scaffolding for the second sister to grow on. Sister number two, beans, remineralizes the soil with nitrogen, an essential component for the other two sisters. And the third sister, squash, takes over the soil, preventing weeds from competing with the first two sisters. The first two sisters, when eaten together, form a complete protein. I'm not sure how, if, or when, but I assume somewhere in there the tomatillo sister fits in, hence the tomatillo milpero.

Sometimes, I struggle to see the point of this knowledge. It's nice to learn about culture, but it's the language that tickles me. Often, learning a new language meant keeping a list of unfamiliar words and later looking them up. In conversation, sometimes asking about a word felt natural, but at other times, I just let them talk without questioning or understanding. Stumbling upon new words serendipitously by being available and playful and present was a joy.

Fluency would be nice. Given enough exposure, over time I'll get there. Even if it means learning Spanish one fart joke at a time.

# Dodson

It's easy for me to forget what food means to people. We were about to close, and one last call-in order was still on the microwave. It had been there for over half an hour, so the food was undoubtedly cold. The lady called in an order every other week. When she had a paper due, she ordered flan, her reward for finishing. I thought she might not show up. No-shows didn't happen often, and when they did, one of us went home with the food.

Despite the current trend, I'm convinced that to-go food isn't as good as the dine-in variety. Much of the time, carry-out leaves the restaurant tepid and arrives at its destination cold. The taste isn't the same as food served hot on a ceramic plate. And the presentation? Forget it. In a take-out box, enchiladas wash around like a ship lost at sea.

Just as we were closing, the lady showed up, and we exchanged smiles. No amount of Styrofoam could have kept her food warm, but she didn't seem to mind. She was chatty and asked how I felt about Curra's, the Mexican restaurant opening directly across the street. Sure, I felt our toes were being stepped on, but the real enemy wasn't another spot selling tacos and ritas. An abandoned building with broken windows across the street would be much worse because one broken window begets another, which leads to boarded-up windows, which lead to graffitied boarded-up windows. It's not a good look for our corner. At least, that's how I made peace with having another Mexican eatery so close.

We didn't talk about broken windows for long. She told me there was a standoff on 35th and MoPac, apparently a hostage situation, and the SWAT team had been called. Street lanes were closed, and the standoff was already hours deep. Someone had gone into a doctor's office with a gun and made a scene. Shootings happened often, and this one was two miles away; I wasn't rattled. I couldn't be the only one desensitized by the frequency of those events.

The next morning was busy with dine-in and to-go orders. Carry-away business used to be peanuts. Now, it's impossible to ignore. I'm not complaining about the sales, but carry-out is the pits. Many eateries now take orders online or with an app, the customer's screen communicating directly with a kitchen printer or screen. One less human, another lost connection.

Preserving personal connections by taking phone orders wasn't much better; bad reception was a test of patience for both parties. In addition to poor reception, the phone made a high-pitched sound to indicate that someone else was on the line. And for a fraction of a second, the phone cut out. That, combined with a rowdy dining room, sometimes phone orders ended in raised voices.

Relying on the phone for to-go orders meant constant interruption. The person who answered the phone also took orders at the register. Sometimes, the queue to the register was all the way to the entrance. The phone rang. "Julio's, can you give me one moment, please?" I put the phone down without waiting for them to answer and finished what I was doing before picking it up. Customers usually waited, but sometimes, when I picked up, I heard a dial tone. To prevent losing a customer on the phone, or worse, a real-life customer in the queue, phone language became scripted. Fluffy words were eliminated. Language was condensed and economized like every movement in the kitchen. After years of stressful rushes, the script became automatic and was used even during slow times.

I was minutes away from finishing my shift. The lion's share of the lunch rush was behind me when the phone rang. Within the first few seconds, I knew the conversation would not follow the script. The lady confessed that she had no idea what to order, but she was feeding many people. Her order was like the Hydra, the mythical serpentine monster whose head multiplied every time it was cut off. Her order multiplied after every question I asked.

"Do you want corn or flour tortillas?"

"I have no idea. Can I get half and half?" I jotted down half corn and half flour.

"Would you like refried beans or charro beans?"

*Beep.*

"I'm sorry, you cut out."

"Would you like refried beans or charro beans?"

"I have no idea. Can I get half and half, please?"

More scribbles.

"And I'm taking this order to two different families. Can you package half the order in one package and the other half in another?" The hydra grew yet another head. In bottled frustration, I tore her order off and scrawled it over again. What I wrote on the notepad and how I wrote it needed to be exact. I wouldn't be around to explain her order to the afternoon crew.

"Can I get a name for the order?"

"Dodson."

I wrote Dodson at the bottom of the ticket, along with the time she would pick up the order and her phone number. She asked if she could pay over the phone. *Beep.* I said yes, entered her credit card information in the terminal, and noted her payment at the bottom of her ticket.

Mom showed up a few minutes later to relieve me. I explained the details of the Dodson order and left.

When I came to work the next day, Mom said, "Hey. Do you remember that large order you took over the phone yesterday? Three chickens cut up with rice and beans?"

My stomach sank. "Yeah. Did everything go out okay?" I worried I'd failed to take the lady's order correctly. One order separated into two boxes, everything half and half, paid over the phone, every special request an opportunity to flub the ticket.

"Everything went out fine. But did you hear about the hostage situation at the pediatrician's office two days ago?"

"Yes."

"Do you remember the name of the order? It was Dodson. Dodson was the name of the doctor who was killed. The order that you took was for that family. Do you know Emily?"

"The nurse practitioner who comes in all the time?"

"Yeah. I think they used to work together. Dodson probably came in a few times with her."

The connection was chilling. I felt a distant tragedy had come disturbingly close. The spirit of the hydra, the order of multiplying details still haunted me. My paranoia escalated. I wondered how I'd come across on the phone. Had I been rude? If I had to ask myself if I'd been rude, I probably was.

I could have been more patient. I could have remembered that food means something different to everyone. With the technological progress the food service industry has made in such a short time, it's easy to forget that food is still about people.

We wrote down the customer's name on phone orders. Dodson was the name I wrote on the bottom of the ticket, a reminder that there is a person on the other end.

# Pelos

While I was still in college, two cooks worked in our kitchen, one on the plancha, the other on the line. They got along better than fine. They had a communication between them, mind to mind, the sort of telepathy that only happens after years of working together. Back then, the kitchen rarely bottlenecked, or maybe I was too green behind the ears to recognize bottlenecks when they occurred.

The planchero had a nickname for everyone, customers and coworkers. He called his fellow cocinero Pelos, which I assumed was because of his mustache. Years after Pelos was gone, I discovered the name referred to the hair on his fingers just beyond the large knuckles. The nickname seemed cruel, though he didn't seem to mind.

One afternoon, I watched Pelos put a taco together for himself. He didn't put meat in it, just a flour tortilla with rice and beans and four or five toppings. He used a flour tortilla because it was bigger and held together better. If you decide to go with corn, make sure you use refried beans instead of charros. The bean juice from the charros will compromise a corn tortilla, so if you go with charros, make sure to tilt the ladle against the tray wall and drain as much juice as possible before adding it to the tortilla. I wasn't the best at draining the bean juice. Not because of poor technique, but I was already salivating when I got to that step and couldn't wait a few more seconds for the bean juice to drain fully.

His taco looked heavenly. After each bite, a little of the filling oozed from the other side of the tortilla and fell on the plate. He needed a spoon. And I needed a taco. I warmed a tortilla on the grill and asked Pelos what he'd put in his. As he rattled off his list, I added copious amounts to my tortilla, folded it, and took my first bite. About half the filling had fallen out by the time I'd eaten through the tortilla; I salvaged the rest with a spoon. Come to think of it, scooping it up with chips would have worked beautifully, as well.

The next day, I wanted the same taco but had only the vaguest idea of how it went. I asked Pelos again, and this time, I counted seven ingredients.

I ate his creation for several days in a row. Then I realized I was so fond of it because it reminded me of my childhood. The taco wasn't his invention but a version of the seven-layer burrito from Taco Bell, which I'd eaten countless times as a kid. I just had to remember the number seven: Spanish rice, charro beans, grated cheese, lettuce, tomato, a dollop of crema, and guacamole. The final ingredient, number eight, was warm tomatillo. It wasn't the same as a seven-layer burrito, but if I had to choose, I liked Pelos's version more.

# Adventure Cost

The community college was in the building where Mom had attended high school decades before. When I registered, I chose to major in biology. On my first day, microbiology was the last class and the worst class of my college career. It wasn't the subject but the poor engagement with which it was taught. I dropped the class after the first exam, and instead of picking another major, I ticked away at core classes I could apply to my four-year degree.

Nothing I studied caught my attention. I lacked conviction about where I wanted to go and what I wanted to do. Desperate for direction, I couldn't help but see my education as anything but a return on investment. You heard it right, the birth of a business major.

I needed to study something that would transfer to the real world, so I concentrated on finance. Economics was part of that path, and I adored it but found it too theoretical, even whimsical. I'm talking about abstractions like the "invisible hand" Adam Smith discussed in his book *The Wealth of Nations*, Ceteris Paribus, the Latin term used in economics to mean "all things remaining the same," and the concept of opportunity cost, the potential benefit missed when choosing one alternative over another.

I transferred to St. Edward's, a small liberal arts school off South Congress Avenue, nothing like the Leviathan University of Texas down the road, which has one of the largest sports arenas in the nation and a billion-dollar gold endowment. St. Edward's lacked UT's resources, but it had a tight community, intimate classes, and professors who kept office hours at the coffee shop on campus. Given my newly adopted, profit-maximizing attitude, I took full advantage of the smaller classes and became one of those eager students who always shot up their hands. I could feel how annoying I was to my peers, but I didn't care.

Of all the courses I took, accounting stuck out. There was nothing special about the sterile room. It was a computer lab with four to six rows of tables. The computer on the desk at the front was hooked up to a projector that displayed its screen. As doldrum as the room was, it was the setting of the most engaging class I took during my college career. No one held a candle to the accounting lab Dr. Harris taught.

The first class was the typical rundown of the syllabus. Dr. Harris told us that he'd started majoring in engineering, struggled, and switched to accounting, graduating with a 4.0 average. I always thought accounting stopped after CPA; Dr. Harris was proof that it went further.

Then Dr. Harris questioned us about ourselves. With some hesitation, I told him and the entire class that I worked at a family restaurant. He'd heard of it and knew where it was. Revealing information about myself was uncharacteristic for me. Such was the power of Dr. Harris's facilitation. He segued into the time he worked at the cafeteria of an all-girls dorm, the most fun job he ever had.

He wasn't so much an accounting instructor as he was a storyteller. His story went like this: Big Boat Builders Inc. needed to hire an intern, you. During your time there, the company frequently found itself in a snafu, and you, the intern, had to come up with a solution to save the day.

During our second class, he presented the company's balance sheet, which was more scrambled than a plate of migas. The challenge was to put it back together. He asked the class questions as he narrated the story. As the plot progressed, we filled in the spreadsheet on our computers, cell by cell. He narrated the story in such a way that as the plot came together, so did the balance sheet. It felt like one of those choose-your-own-adventure games, with the evil winged dragons replaced by heinous notes payable.

The second adventure was a review of BBB's income statement. For one hour each week, we hacked away at the numbers. The company was always in trouble, and the intern always had the answer. One of the hairier conundrums was inventory, the cursed FIFO LIFO lesson: first in, first out vs last in, first out. How counting could ever be so complicated could only be explained by someone who did it for a living. Dr. Harris wielded the torch of insight, shining light on the matter and helping us interns navigate the warren of numbers.

The final quest was a honker of a problem set with multiple spreadsheets. It took up the whole class and went from top to bottom of everything we'd learned that semester. By the nature of the problem, I knew this would be our last quest together as a class.

"Good job, intern," Harris told us. "You saved the BBB from another disaster. And you made it to the end of your internship." He let the good vibes ring for a moment.

"But the phone rings. It's the CEO. He wants you in his office. He was impressed by your effort and wants to offer you a full-time position." He paused. "But there's a catch: the office he wants you to work from is in Germany. That's right, Germany, where it's cold for half the year and far from your family and friends. But this is your first real job, the first time you'll have your own place and money to buy your own things. And the CEO needs an answer by the end of the week."

Dr. Harris walked around the desk at the front of the class as if to give us time to process the opportunity. "Do you take the job?"

My hand popped up like water off boiling oil. "Yes! Take the job and have an adventure."

Dr. Harris smiled. Other students agreed and wanted to make the trip to Germany.

We were approaching the end of the year, and it was time to enroll for the next semester. I looked up the classes Dr. Harris taught. They were all upper-division accounting classes reserved for accounting majors. I contemplated switching my major just to take more of his classes.

I finished school without hiccups. I never became the intern who got the job, nor did I go to Germany. I stayed at the restaurant and kept chugging along, doing the same things.

One evening, in the gap between the dinner rush and closing, Dr. Harris walked in. I was out of my skin with excitement and took his order personally— nachos and another plate to-go. While he was in front of me, a peculiar feeling ensnared me. The joy of seeing my favorite professor deflated. We didn't talk much. He ordered and took a seat opposite the register while he waited for his food.

I don't recall much about inventory or cash flows. A common sentiment among businesspeople is, "I wish I'd paid more attention in accounting class." I remembered Dr. Harris's class, though. At the end of his class, when it was time to go to Germany and have an adventure, my hand shot up, and with great gusto, I exclaimed, "Yes!" Yet here I was, years later, doing the same thing I did when I took his class.

I went back to the kitchen, out of sight, and waited for the cheese to melt on his nachos. There was no internship, no job in Germany. For a long time, I pondered the potential benefit, the price I'd paid for choosing one adventure over another.

# Chivo

've always been a sucker for popular trends. My latest is turning off all notifications on my phone except calls and texts. In no time, the low-interruption diet was such a success, I applied it to other distractions. I checked my mailbox once a month and replied to emails only when I had to.

We received a letter in the mail from the city. They were implementing a strategy whereby restaurants disposed of organic waste separately. Food scraps, paper products, and leftovers from plates needed their own bin. URGENT letters kept coming in, and I kept ignoring them. After a couple of months, Mom handed me a letter stamped FINAL NOTICE.

"Have you done this yet?" she asked.

I shook my head.

"We need to do this tomorrow."

Finding a compost company was a first for me. I had zero idea what to look for, so I typed the keywords into the browser and went down the list. One of the compost companies I found used words like "innovative" and "disruptive" to describe their services as if they had invented composting. I emailed the first three or four providers, minus the disruptors, and went with the first business that wrote back.

At first, I was skeptical about separating every bit of food waste. I purchased a green bin from the restaurant supply and told the crew to put the organic waste in it. Our first load was mainly fruit and vegetable peels and chicken bones. The green bin was so hefty it required two people to toss it into the barrel by the dumpsters. The sloshing sound the waste made when it hit the bottom was both repulsive and satisfying.

As the weeks went by, for some unknown reason, the green bin got lighter and lighter until I could toss it without help. A separate bag of vegetable peelings was kept by the back door. When I asked why, one of the workers confessed that it was para los chivos. Monserrat kept goats at home and wanted to feed them our scraps. Some days, they'd go wild and eat them all, other days, not a bite. She called the goats mañosos, capricious. We joked that the scraps were going toward our Christmas barbacoa feast.

Christmas came and went. We didn't get the barbacoa dinner we thought we'd earned.

One day, she brought us a plastic bowl filled with homemade goat cheese, but only a few of us tried it. Some claimed they didn't like goat cheese or made another excuse. Cocina politics, if you ask me.

Monserrat loved to talk about her chivos. She told me about a man in Hutto who specialized in everything chivo. He sold goats, cleaned them, and skinned them. "And he does subastas, too. Do you know what subastas are?"

"No. What are they?"

She described an auction. "¿Sabes qué? The other day, he sold us two goats, one male and one female. The female was chaparrita y gordita. Short and fat. The man who sold them told me he'd never seen la gordita with chivos and assumed that she only liked the company of other chivas."

"How many chivos do you have now?"

"Ten, and you know, since it hasn't rained lately, it can be expensive to feed them. If there is no grass for them to eat, we have no choice but to buy feed. They love it. I think there's something in it that makes it sweet. You know what happened today? As I was feeding them, I counted them. I only counted nine. I thought it was strange, so I went around the corner looking for la gordita, and guess what? We have another chivo!"

"Really? That makes eleven chivos."

"Right."

"I guess she doesn't only like chivas."

One day, Monserrat asked, "Are you working Thursday night?"

"Yes."

"Ok. We'll make barbacoa."

"¿De chivo?"

"De chivo."

That Thursday, she brought a massive olla containing a prepped and seasoned chivo. She put it on the corner burner and cooked it for a few hours during the dinner rush. She said she was cooking it al vapor, steaming it.

At the end of the shift, she pulled out tender chunks of rib meat, warmed up a few corn tortillas, and laid the feast on a table family-style with red and green salsas. I took a chip and dipped it in both salsas. The red salsa was so spicy I instantly got the hiccups. Everybody laughed when I warned them about how spicy it was. Nearly everyone ate the chivo and burned the hell out of themselves with red salsa.

There was nothing disruptive or innovative about the chivo organic waste plan. But the red salsa was quite disruptive. Spicy salsa always gives me the hiccups.

# Mex-Tex

On Fridays after work, I often had margaritas with a couple of friends. Nothing fancy. At the peak of summer, they'd come out of the machine completely liquid, on the rocks minus the rocks, but what can you expect from a rita that costs less than five bucks?

Every three or four outings, we'd discuss Mexican food – the places I should visit the next time I was in Mexico, specifically Guadalajara, where they were from. This time, the chat veered into adjacent territory: Mexican food in Texas.

I was surprised to hear they had a soft spot for Tex-Mex. They thought Tex-Mex was authentic – not a cuisine trying to be something it wasn't or a cheap imitation of Mexican food, but its own thing.

One of my buddies worked at the café when Papá was still the owner. The other visited a couple of times, maybe only once, and confessed he'd had our frozen rita but never eaten our food. He asked, "Do you consider Julio's food Mexican or Tex-Mex?"

My friend's question stumped me. I fumbled and froze.

After working for three or so years as a computer programmer, Papá had his fill of cubicle life and thought opening a restaurant was his best way out. No one in Austin was selling rotisserie chicken at the time, so he borrowed a few thousand dollars from his suegra, Mamá Abuela, and started selling caribe-style chicken, using a recipe heavily influenced by how chickens were roasted in Venezuela.

But I couldn't tell my friend we served Venezuelan food, because the Venezuela theme didn't go further than the chicken. As a kid, I asked Papá why the restaurant didn't sell arepas. "They're too labor intensive," he said. "No one wants to eat an arepa when they can buy a hamburger for the same price." Mamà Abuela also contributed her rice and beans recipes, which weren't the typical caribe-style black beans and white rice, but Spanish rice and pinto beans, more Tex-Mex or Mexican, the difference being the amount of cumin. If you want Mexican rice, a three-fingered pinch of comino will do. If you want Tex-Mex rice, use cumin by the fistful.

The café started selling chalupas too, our version of the tostada. Unlike caribe-style rotisserie chicken, the café was not the first to sell tostadas in Austin. So we made ours unique. Mamá Abuela went against the grain and made the tostadas from flour tortillas instead of corn, which classified them as Tex-Mex. But she was no dummy. A tostada made from a flour tortilla produces a flakey shell, not crunchy like a traditional corn tortilla. If making a tostada with a flour tortilla instead of a corn tortilla categorizes the dish as Tex-Mex, I get it. But if a Mexican-born cook creates the recipe, does that make it Mexican?

Mexican cuisine has deep traditional roots, but it's also highly creative. Does using a flour tortilla cross that line? I wish I'd mentioned these things when my friend asked what I thought our food was.

When the restaurant migrated from its first location, we acquired more space and expanded our menu. Instead of just offering tacos for breakfast, we now offered classic plates: migas, huevos rancheros, huevos a la Mexicana, and safer options, like eggs with toast and French toast. Breakfast tacos were more popular north of the border than south of it. Breakfast tacos in Mexico were tacos al vapor, steamed. They were delicious, but north of the border, a taco al vapor would not be considered a breakfast taco, a taco de huevo.

Huevos rancheros and huevos a la Mexicana are common breakfast plates in Mexico, while I guess migas are more commonly Tex-Mex. Or at least the style we served were. Our recipe called for scrambled eggs with tomatoes, onions, cilantro, fried corn tortilla bits, and cheddar cheese. That isn't to say that migas isn't Mexican, but plenty of places in Texas serve them and serve them well.

Papá continued to fill in the menu. Mamá Abuela's enchiladas verdes held the throne as the most popular item. Second place went to her caldo de pollo, not to be confused with the red-broth chicken tortilla soup. Instead, ours was a clear-broth, abuelita-style caldo de pollo. I consider both dishes Mexican, although we preferred the melting qualities of jack cheese on the enchiladas instead of the traditional queso fresco. Then we added beef, chicken, and veggie quesadillas. Guacamole, which I consider Mexican, was also added. It is made with avocado, onion, cilantro, tomato, and salt, no dairy. However, next to the guacamole was queso, the hallmark of Tex-Mex cuisine. The only way to get more Tex-Mex was with chili con carne cheese enchiladas, which we did not serve. I could just hear my friend now.

As the years went by, our nachos morphed from individual style to pile style. For a time, Papá drew deep inspiration from a restaurant he frequented and added Caesar salad to the menu. Ironically, Caesar salad can be considered Mexican because it was invented in Tijuana, although the man who created it was Italian. It was never popular on our menu, and eventually, Papá dropped it.

Just before Mom took over, Papá jumped the hoops and invested in a liquor license to serve margaritas. From my experiences, micheladas were ubiquitous in Mexico, mountains more popular than margaritas. Papá also offered a Mexican martini, which is not Mexican but a cocktail uniquely from Austin. All three drinks lived harmoniously on our menu.

When Mom got behind the wheel, she added carne guisada, beef stew, to the menu. Initially, it wasn't popular, but it gained a following over the years. I never gravitated toward guisada. When I was a kid, we used to eat tons of carne mechada, a Venezuelan dish I assume Papá taught Mom to make. The taste and sauces are similar, but carne mechada is made with shredded beef, while guisada is made with stew meat. Did our interpretation of guisada make it less Tex-Mex and more Ven-Tex-Mex? Years later, one of the cooks added her twist to the dish: chipotle peppers. Not many, just a few. Does adding chipotle peppers to carne guisada change the dish's identity again?

The restaurant has never been a cultural statement. It was Papá's parachute out of the office, a vehicle to showcase Mamá Abuela's cooking and a way to earn a living. We added menu items that would sell while preserving Mamà Abuela's recipes. Borders, definitions, and identity were consigned to the backseat.

Authentic? I don't know what that word means anymore. All I know is that when I came into work in the afternoon, Mom often grabbed a booth in the corner and ate a corn tortilla with rice and beans, lettuce and tomatoes, a scoop of guacamole, some chicken, and maybe a handful of chips. She ate what she sold. And at the end of our shift, the staff and I also ate the food.

Getting back to my friend's question, I had no idea if our menu could be classified as Tex-Mex. Like many other restaurants in the area, we offered both cuisines. To answer him honestly, I'd have to come up with terms, definitions, and family identity.

I began to answer and immediately tied up. My friend noticed.

"It's not Tex-Mex," he said, "it's Mex-Tex."

We all laughed. Next time I'm asked, I might just stick with that.

# Side Hustle

I was talking with a friend about work culture.

"¿Cómo se dice 'side hustle' en Español?" I inquired, curious how the idea was converted to Spanish.

"¿Qué es un side hustle?" he asked.

"Un side hustle es un trabajo que tienes además que tu otro trabajo," I replied, explaining that it was a second job in addition to one's main job. "Muchas veces es un trabajo más pequeño, y más sencillo."

He furrowed his brow and paused. "¿Pues se llama trabajo, no?" It's still called a job, right?

His response wasn't what I was looking for. I had sought to learn more Spanish and more about Mexican culture. Instead, I learned more about my own.

# Shampoo

The running joke was that winter in Austin only lasted a couple of weeks. During those few frigid days, feel-good recipes wriggled out of the crew. Caldo de res had the throne, no comparison in flavor or body sensation. If you can think of another food that raises the hairs on the back of your head like beef broth, please let me know. One of my dear friends from Guadalajara said they called it cocido or cocido de res.

A cold snap exacerbated the afternoon lull. The planchero asked for money to get milk from the grocery store across the street, which was odd because he was *never* one to fetch anything. A gallon of milk and half an hour later, everyone in the back was drinking hot chocolate. I don't have much of a sweet tooth, and I'd already poured myself a mug of coffee. "No gracias," I replied. "I don't want chocolate."

"No es chocolate," Antonia shot back, "es champurrado."

I struggled to keep track of the names of the creations that came out of the kitchen. It was obviously good. Everyone had a tall cup full of the sweet warmth, and consensus within the crew was rare.

The midafternoon slump stretched into the evening. The dinner rush was just a whimper. My mug of coffee was long gone. Chilly and bored, I needed an evening lift. Brewing a pot of joe for just one mug seemed wasteful. I asked if any of the drink they'd made was still around. I had already forgotten the name.

"Champurrado. We still have some if you want," Isabel replied.

"¿Shampoo qué?" It sounded like they were saying shampoo with an ado ending.

"Cham ... Pu ... RRa ... Do," Antonia said. I didn't care if she was being rude. I wanted to try some and to be warm. I repeated the word. "¿Cham ... Pu ... Ra ... Do?"

"RRa, RRa, Rra ... Do. Cham ... Pu ... *Rra* ... Do."

"Cham ... Pu ... *Rra* ... Do," I repeated, forcing the rolling Rs.

"Yes."

"And what's in it?"

"Milk, chocolate, maíz, cinnamon, vanilla. Normally piloncillo, but we don't have any." It was in a repurposed bulk sour cream container with a handleless Styrofoam cup floating on top as a ladle. I grabbed a clean mug and served myself. Even without the piloncillo, the Mexican brown sugar, it was as sweet as I'd expected. Whatever it took to keep my bones from rattling was fine with me.

The next day, I worked the lunch shift and told the crew about my experience with champurrado. I asked if they'd ever heard of it. They said something about atole, which wasn't the same. Mom used to make atolito for us when we were kids: oatmeal made soupy with a healthy serving of milk and sometimes butter. But the sweet cocoa corn drink I'd had the night before was nothing like the oatmeal Mom made to keep us warm.

"Not atole," I said defiantly. "Atole, you eat with a spoon. Champurrado is a drink, like hot chocolate, but with maíz."

The crew turned toward me with bent brows. "You don't eat atole," one replied, "you drink it. It is a beverage, espeso, made with maíz." Thick, made with corn.

"Yes, champurrado, you drink. Mom made atole for us as kids. And we ate it with a spoon."

"Perdón. But I've never seen anyone eat atole with a spoon. You're confusing it with something else."

I searched the web for an answer to our dispute. The evening crew called it champurrado; the morning crew called it atole, and the oatmeal Mom made us as kids was atolito. I was not wrong about this. They were.

When the search result popped up, I turned away from the crew. "¡Ya ves!" they howled. "What does it say?"

"Nada."

"¡A ver!" the cocinera giggled, peeking at my phone, which showed pictures of the warmth from the evening prior.

Atole, also atol, is similar to champurrado. And nothing like oatmeal. Years, decades of using the wrong word. Why would Mom call oatmeal atole? How was I supposed to know about food and culture with mixed terminology?

My ignorance made sense after the fact. Oats were not native to Mexico, unlike corn and chocolate. Atol was probably more Mexican than Tequila. My mind, prematurely and with no evidence, jumped to an abuelita five hundred years ago, pulverizing corn and cocoa in a mortero.

It's been decades since Mom made us oatmeal. We had it so much as kids, I don't miss it as an adult. I've had enough for a lifetime. However, unlike the food itself, I'm fond of my memories of oatmeal. I wouldn't mind reliving those chilly days.

There were more frigid days ahead. The evening crew kept making atol/champurrado, or whatever you want to call the stuff made with chocolate and maíz. They'd ask if I wanted some. I'd say yes, and they'd fill a sixteen-ounce to-go cup to the brim for me. Sometimes, it was really corny, sometimes chocolatey, and almost always too sweet. At the most, I drank half of what I was served. As a kid, I'd overdone atolito. I didn't want to overdo champurrado, too.

# Natural Waters

Two guys walked in. One clean cut, the other with long hair, neck and hand tattoos, and a gold cuerno de chivo necklace. They barely looked at the menu before ordering. Clean cut did the talking.

"Two enchiladas, please."

"Two plates?"

"Yeah," he paused. "They come with rice and beans?"

"Yes."

He looked past me at the refrigerator.

"What do you have to drink? Do you have natural waters?" I assumed he was a Spanish speaker. '¿Qué aguas naturales tienen?' sounds better, or '¿Que aguas tienen?' I understand all three.

I get the question all the time. Do we have horchata or jamaica or something like naranjada? The lavatrastes makes agua de limón y pepino– cucumber limeade. One glass and you feel like you're eighteen again. She only makes enough for the kitchen, though. A saying I made up: primero los dientes, luego los clientes – first teeth, later clients. Bastardized from the original: primero los dientes, luego los parientes – first teeth, later family members.

"We only have limonada."

"Is it natural?"

"Agua, limón, azúcar." I said to him in Spanish, again, assuming he was a speaker.

"Give me two Jarritos."

I opened the fridge, grabbed two fruit punches, and cracked open both bottles. I've heard people call Coke agua, but by no means would I call it natural. Clean cut paid for everything. Not a word from the long hair.

# Away

Toward the beginning of her tenure, Mom put a bench on the corner. Technically, the tiny strip was city property, but since nothing was being done with the land, she took the liberty of installing it between two trees, one of which was a mulberry.

The bench was an instant hit. One of the regulars was an older man with a beard more or less the same shape and size as Santa's, though not winter white. His was stained yellow, maybe from all the sunlight he got. It could have been from coffee. More than likely, it was from copious amounts of malt liquor.

For the sake of confidentiality, we'll call the man Jay. It was no coincidence that of all the benches in Austin, Jay chose that bench. The adjacent trees provided an abundant canopy, and two bus stops were within one block. The people of Hyde Park were mostly sympathetic. Best of all, he could solicit from three patios and several nearby businesses. Our patio wasn't only the largest one. It was also the patio closest to Jay's bench.

It wasn't long before we caught onto his strategy. He'd walk through our patio asking patrons for spare change, cross the parking lot, tag the patio next door, loop around the building, and hit up the third patio on the other side, next to the bakery. From there, he would either cross the street and make a round at the grocery store or complete his loop by returning to the bench. His laps were often fruitful; when they weren't, he'd take a breather at the bench before making another lap. Eventually, he'd make his way to the bus stop and leave. Sometimes, he returned to the bench with a little brown paper bag, perhaps with more dye to paint his beard.

Jay asking patrons for spare change was a bad look for the business. The next time he approached our customers, we intervened. When we saw him lift himself from the bench, we stood outside by the front door or against the fence as if to say, "I see you. Don't bug our customers." He often pretended not to see us, skipped our patio, and went to the next one. Sometimes, customers gave him a box of leftover food instead of money. His interest in leftovers was inconsistent. Sometimes, he took a bite or two; other times, he set the box aside and kept going.

Jay dragged his feet, which made him a cinch to spot, often many paces before he reached our patio. What he lacked in speed, he made up for in tenacity. During the rush, we were too busy to keep an eye on him. He'd be halfway down the patio with his hand extended before we saw him. I'd excuse myself from our customers and run him off. Regardless of how many times we asked him not to come by, he kept returning.

Usually, you can put a spin on any situation, fabricate a lesson, or find virtue in a negative event. Not with Jay. It was a sunk experience, a total loss with no redeemable quality. And while I would never wish ill on anyone, I wished he would go away. I didn't know or care where, just *away*.

We weren't the only ones who struggled with Jay's persistence. The bakery and coffee shop and the trattoria across the street grappled with him, as well. We all knew his situation was beyond the limits of our imaginations. No one wanted Jay to experience more harm than he already had. With that said, the only way to manifest our collective wish was to call the cops.

Half the time the cops were called, they couldn't find him. He'd somehow manage to dodder away just in time. And even if the cops apprehended him, they rarely took him away. When they did, he'd be gone for a day or two max before he was back at his favorite bench.

One evening, we found that someone had relieved themselves in one of our planters with only the moon as a witness. At most, the planter was only a handful of yards from the bench. I thought it must have been Jay. I went out of my way to be friendly or at least neutral toward everyone else.

Around that time, Jay had the bolas to enter the café while I was busy in the back, and when I looked around, I saw him leaving the restroom. My stomach sank. Surely, he'd left cave drawings on the walls, but to my surprise, the restroom was fine.

My intention was always to remain firm with Jay, though as time went by, the hairs on my tongue began to thin. My words became less filtered, and my attitude drifted below neutral. One day, I saw him moving down our patio, although no one was dining there. I yanked open the front door and was behind him before he could exit. I found him hunched over the ground. He turned around, opened his hand, and mumbled softly—something about cigarette butts. The few butts in his hand had been smoked to the filter, barely a nip of tobacco left, but enough to make them worth bending over.

Not long after, Mom came up to me and said calmly, "Don't kick someone when they're down."

"I'm not kicking anyone. I'm being firm with him." By that time, my game of cat-and-mouse with Jay had gone on and off for years. Sometimes, it was every day. I don't remember if Mom said anything else, but she didn't have to.

One afternoon, as I walked past Jay, he turned to me and began to mumble. He mumbled often, and I never hung around to listen, but this time, I engaged. His bloodshot eyes were hard to look at, so I looked down at his shoes instead. Lumps of quiet words came out of his mouth, inconsistent snippets of meaning. "Check every month ...

two weeks ... run out, ask for money." I raised my eyes from his shoes and looked at his blood-shot eyes, his raw cheeks, his dyed beard.

Like most barrio chisme, gossip about Jay was inconsistent and unreliable. One rumor was that he suffered from a wave of divergence not even his family could manage. Another was that he was once in the military, hence the monthly check. The most far-fetched rumor was that back in the day, he'd been given a lobotomy. The only thing I knew for certain was what I heard him say that day and what I witnessed with my own eyes.

Years later, out of nowhere, I noticed Jay finally disappeared. I asked Mom if she knew anything about him. "Oh, you didn't hear?" she asked. Jay went away. Far, far away.

# San Martín

"Hijos de su Madre!" What Rogelio really said was more colorful. "Look at all these people without masks, as if nothing is happening." All of us in the kitchen looked out at the street. "They are outside, though," I said.

"I don't care. They're breathing all over the place, spreading the virus everywhere."

"But they're outside. The risk isn't the same outside as it is inside."

"¡A mi me vale! They should all be inside, not jogging outside, contagiando a todos." The others looked at the joggers and nodded in solidarity. "We're in lockdown, but these people go out running without a mask." Rogelio began to mock the joggers, prancing in place, taking shallow steps, his wrists limp. "If I were in charge, I would send the police and round up anyone without permission to leave their house," he commanded, index finger pointing in different directions as if he were a captain giving orders. "¡A la casa!" Another string of curse words followed. Rogelio transitioned between moods fluidly. His language gave no clues to his real emotion, and his vulgarities indicated only that he was feeling something without revealing what it was.

Rogelio soon cooled down, propped his phone against the dishes, and focused on the news. It was all numbers, maps, and graphs. He seemed to be as informed as anyone, way more informed than I was. I didn't know up from down and had no idea what to believe.

Business was dead, so I didn't object when he glued himself to his phone. My silence was permission for others to do the same. With nothing left to do until we served dinner, I sat in one of the booths by the window and waited for the phone to ring, watching the maskless world go by. It seemed as though they were all exercising, walking, or jogging. If the pandemic was good for anything, it made for better people-watching.

Antonia came in a little later than everyone else because she had to drive up from her other job in South Austin. She usually made it to the café just as the last batch of chickens came out of the rotisserie. More often than not, Rogelio had them on the countertop by the time she arrived.

After clocking in and wrapping herself in a mandil, she eyeballed the chickens and picked the birds with the best skin texture, size, and color. Those were sold as quarters, halves, and wholes. The rest were pulled apart and used in other dishes.

I often heard Antonia punch her timecard from across the café, but that day, she walked straight past the chickens to the dining area, pulled a chair up to the front door, stepped on it, and placed a couple of plastic ramekins containing water and chopped lettuce on the top of the door frame. Just above the door, Aunt Bobbie had mounted a card to the window depicting a soldier on horseback about to slice his cloak in half and share it with a shivering old man.

I'm familiar with Catholic prayer cards. In Latin America, I often see La Virgin de Guadalupe pegged to the center console of buses and taxis. It's impossible not to notice the cards while bombing down a serpentine mountain road. Just as I became comfortable with my own death, I'd casually wonder how fast the vehicle was traveling, only to find La Virgin tacked over the speedometer.

I remember seeing a prayer card in Mama Abuela's kitchen drawer – either the drawer with all the rubber bands or the one with the saved grocery bags. We never had those cards in our house, nor that many saved plastic bags. There was a gap between us, a bridge missing, an unshared sense of spirituality.

The next day, it happened again. Antonia punched her timecard and wrapped an apron around her waist, but instead of tending to the chickens, she grabbed a chair to stand on and swapped out the ramekins from the previous day, replenished the day-old water and replaced the dehydrating lettuce with cool, crisp leaves.

I'd paid no mind the first time, but now she had my attention. She dipped her finger in the water and rubbed it on the horse's mouth, then did the same with the lettuce. "Pobrecito," I heard her say, "no one here gives you food or water." Antonia sensed I was watching. "One day, we won't give him any water. See how he likes it."

"Why are you dipping your finger in the water and lettuce and rubbing it on the horse's mouth?" I asked.

"Es pasto. To show him where the food and water are."

"But you put the water in front of him. Isn't that enough?"

"No, you have to show him where it is." She stepped down from the chair, put it back against the table, and went to the chickens. I took a moment to look at the card and the replenished containers.

"What is San Martín the saint of?"

"You should know this by now," Antonia said. "Look it up on your phone."

I opened the browser on my phone and began typing San Martín de Porres. I read the answer aloud to Antonia as she pulled the chickens off the skewers and prepped them for the evening.

"San Martín de Porres is the saint–"

"No es él," she interrupted.

"It's not San Martín de Porres?"

"No," she said, as if I'd committed another offense.

I backspaced "de Porres." I remembered hearing the crew talk about Martín Caballero, but I thought they were talking about the husband of a cocinera called Martín.

I typed in caballero, and San Martín Caballero came up. He was the saint of the needy, gambling, and shopkeepers. That made more sense.

"He is the saint of necessity, stores, and business," I reported. "It says he's popular in Mexico."

"He is very important to us."

Antonia didn't make offerings to San Martín every day. If we were already busy when she clocked in, she'd hurry to her station and got straight to work. Other times, I'm sure she just forgot. If she missed several consecutive days, the ramekin of water evaporated, and the lettuce dried up.

I used to question religion, prod, and play with it. Not maliciously, just for the sake of swinging words around, oblivious to how they landed. Sometimes, a conversation about religion would arise in the kitchen. They'd talk. I'd say something, the wrong thing, and they'd get quiet. I learned just to listen.

Believing is a personal business, especially when peppered with uncertainty. Say what you will, I had a hard time buying in. I found it difficult to believe that prosperity would magically land on the restaurant if we simply made an offering to San Martín. I didn't object to leaving a couple of saucers for Saint Martín's horse. Once or twice, it was me standing on the chair placing fresh water and pasto on the door frame. But I didn't dip my finger into the water and rub it on the horse's mouth. If he wanted to eat and drink, that was up to him.

# Machete Fest

pulled up to the dish pit with a bin full of dirty dishes, plopped it, and turned to Agustín. "Hay fiesta hoy." There's a party today.

"¡A huevo!" he said. "Let's go."

"Do you know where Travis Heights is?"

"No."

"It's south of the river, but not that far. We can ride bikes."

"Órale, vamos."

The day Agustìn started at the café, I introduced myself and asked where he was from. He said Guadalajara. The only thing I knew about Guadalajara was Las Chivas, their wildly popular soccer team. In an attempt to connect, I asked if he was a Chivas fan. He was the first Mexican I'd met who didn't like fútbol much. He said he liked to patinar instead. When I asked, he made it clear he meant skateboarding.

When we were teens, my cousin and I poked around our neighborhoods searching for places to skateboard, specifically churches and schools where he could grind low ledges and ollie down stairs. Agustín and I talked about ledges and jumping stairs. When I asked how many stairs he could ollie, he gave me a bemused look. "¿Cuántas escaleras?"

"Sí. ¿Cuántas escaleras? How many stairs have you ollied?"

He informed me that escaleras were a set of stairs and that an escalón was one step, one stair. "¿Cuántos escalones?" was the correct way to ask. I rephrased my question.

Agustín's answer was impressive. People don't ollie that many stairs by accident. Which is partially why I thought rolling up to the party by bike was a brilliant idea. Skating and cycling have a lot in common. Both involve traveling on wheels and weaving through urban landscapes.

Before heading to the party, we would have to ask Agustín's roommate if he could borrow his bike. They were childhood friends, so borrowing his bike wouldn't be an issue. We were forty-something blocks north of the river, and the shindig was many blocks south of the river. I thought that wasn't too far by bike, though it might be for someone who didn't cycle as frequently as I did. Agustín once showed me a video of him pulling off a 360 Flip. Anyone who could pull off a move like that was athletic. He'd be fine.

We had something else in common. He was hungry for English and I wanted to beef up my Spanish. He spoke to me in English, and I volleyed back in Spanish. If he made a mistake, I corrected him, and he did the same for me, though never in an overbearing way. We got awkward looks because our communication sounded like a hodgepodge to other people.

From the restaurant to Townlake was mostly downhill. We rode through Hyde Park to North Campus, the university, then uphill for a couple of blocks passing the capitol, and downhill through downtown. The river, a block beyond, was more or less the midpoint, though if measured by effort, it still wasn't quite halfway.

A few blocks south of the river, the first big hill was just ahead of us. Halfway up, I heard Agustín mumble, "No mames." No way! The hill went on for many blocks. We got off the main road and took a left into the dark neighborhood. Travis Heights was known for its majestic live oaks and rolling hills. We encountered another hill and another, and with each one came another "No mames." Agustín asked if we were almost there.

"Almost. After the highway, just a couple more blocks, and that's it." Those last two blocks were a doozy, the steepest uphill of the whole journey.

The party was at a house rented by a few friends, all of them girls, and I had a crush on one of them. Predictably, they'd primarily invited guys, making the ratio favorable to the girls. I was oblivious to the imbalance until we were in the garage playing ping pong, and Agustín leaned in. "Carnal, where are the girls? There are only guys here."

"Sí hay chicas," I countered.

"Yeah, the girl you like." I looked around. He was right. Only one girl was playing ping-pong with us; the rest were guys.

"This is a sausage fest," Agustìn blurted out.

"¿Dónde aprendiste eso?" Where did you learn that?

"From Diego."

"¿Y cómo se dice sausage fest en Español?" How do you say sausage fest in Spanish? I knew for certain it wasn't fiesta de chorizo.

"Puro machete."

"¿Por qué puro machete?" Why pure machete?

"En México, en los pueblos y las cantinas, you see men walk around with machetes strapped to their hips."

"¿En las cantinas?" I asked in awe.

"Yes. They carry their machetes into the cantinas." A dim cantina came to mind. Glowing amber lanterns, wooden chairs, wooden tables, wooden everything, and a bunch of men with machetes.

"Entonces, ¿esta fiesta es puro machete?" So, this party is pure machete? I asked, solidifying my new vocab.

"Simón. This is a sausage fest."

Maybe a beer later, I noticed that Agustín had been struck by a fit of sneezes. He said he was allergic to cats. There was a cat in the house, as if the machetes hadn't been enough. We had to get out of there.

Our bike ride home was silent. Uphill into Travis Heights, downhill to the river, then gradually uphill to Hyde Park. Agustín wasn't familiar with Austin yet. I rode past where I lived to where he was staying. He barely said goodbye when we parted ways.

Idiot me, I should have known better. I had lungs for days but only brains for minutes. A nighttime bike cruise for me was VO2 max training for my non-cyclist amigo.

Thankfully, Agustín didn't hold a grudge. Over the years, we've been to more fiestas than two whippersnappers could count. If the party was in the neighborhood, we rolled up by bike. If it was south of the river, we went by car. Sometimes, we stumbled upon a fiesta with cats. Other times, none at all.

# El Churr

Soon after we hired Mauricio, he left but returned a year and some change later. When he came back, we were desperate for extra muscle, and he was desperate for the hours. He didn't mind working every day, including weekends. On Saturdays, he showed up early and stayed until closing. Many new hires are that eager when they first start. Mauricio wanted to prove himself. He caught on so quickly, it was as if he'd never left.

One of the many sayings that stuck in the kitchen was "sure." Mom started it. There's nothing special about the word, but she didn't say it in the normal way. It sounded like "'surrre," with an emphasis on the "sh" sound and with a heavy R. It sounded silly because it *was* silly, but we did things like that to make work feel less like work. The others started to imitate her, not in a bad way. We all tend to repeat what we hear. Because Mauricio was so eager to learn and fit in, he began saying "surrre" when anyone asked him for help.

"¿Me puedes rallar queso?" Can you grate cheese for me? "Surrre."

"¿Me puedes ayudar en los trastes?" Can you help me with the dishes? "Surrre." Though he never really said 'surrre,' when he said it, it sounded more like 'churr.' I'm guessing the "ch" sound was easier for him to make. Mauricio said churr so often that a couple of the cocineras started calling him El Churr. We all laughed about it because when you're busy as hell, what else is there to laugh at but senseless, made-up jokes?

At the café, the life span of jokes and sayings phased in and out. Eventually, they stopped calling Mauricio El Churr so often. Maybe the joke had run its course. Or perhaps they stopped calling him that because he stopped saying churr to everything they asked of him.

# Buttons

Some of our customers liked that we were cash-only. I heard it quite often. One guy called it Julio's money. "This is the only place I still use cash," he joked. A breakfast place down the street was also cash-only. After decades at the same location, modern Austin forced them to relocate, and thankfully they did. But when they opened in their new location, they started accepting cards.

Being a cash-only business had a certain mystique, like we were washing money or something, which couldn't have been further from the truth. Mom, Papá, and I were goody two-shoes. Just ask our accountant.

We had a sign on the front door: "Cash only. Thanks for understanding." As I stood at the register, watching through the glass, I'd often see new customers' faces scrunch up as they read the sign. They'd consult each other, then turn away.

Although we lost business, being cash-only had its advantages. The people who came went to the trouble of carrying cash because they really wanted to be there. Our regulars were like broken in boots, familiar and pleasant to interact with.

In an age of tablets and touch screens, our behemoth register was more appropriate to a museum than a modern business. We didn't mind the machine's bulkiness because that made it robust and reliable. We didn't mind losing business because we weren't equipped to take credit cards. The register never froze, never a glitch, which was great for business. Plus, this living relic had buttons. Nothing has buttons anymore.

There was no guessing how long the pandemic would last. It could have been weeks or years. Either way, it didn't take long for other businesses to adapt. Curbside services sprang up. Partnerships between restaurants and food delivery services solidified. QR codes replaced laminated menus, and online ordering made servers and cashiers redundant.

Credit cards had a wavy, WiFi-looking symbol on them, signifying they were capable of contactless payment, and phones stored card information—no touching necessary. We remained obstinate, heels firmly planted in the earth. Papá loved to say cash is king—cold, hard cash.

Cash had a bad rap, and with the pandemic, it worsened. "You don't know where that dollar's been," people loved to say. Customers started handling cash with latex gloves or stuffed it into Ziploc sandwich bags or envelopes. "No change back, thank you," they said, doubling both as precaution and propina.

Remaining cash-only wasn't about sidestepping the banks or fees. Nor did we believe that cash was a superior form of payment. Mom avoided technology, and to a lesser extent, so did I. When I mentioned accepting cards, she told me how much trouble the coffee shop next door had when the internet went down.

I understood her point of view. She was guerrera. Sometimes, the electricity at the café went out for a few hours, but Mom didn't skip a beat. She grabbed a calculator and notepad for payments, lit a few candles, and served most of the menu, no problem. The grill ran on gas, the rotisserie too, though the skewers had to be turned by hand. In those moments, no one flinched. She thought a system reliant on the internet would be too fragile. What would we do if the electricity went out?

Power outages or not, change was inevitable. Not even our "cash is king" battle cry could save us. Magic wand money was a breeze, and tapping and hearing that dopamine ding added to the addiction. Convenient payment methods were here to stay.

A few months into the pandemic, a young lady called in an order for carry-out—a beef quesadilla and something else, queso or guacamole. I didn't bother to tell her we were cash-only. We'd been cash-only for thirty-seven years, so I thought people knew. When she came in, I rang her up, and she pulled out her card.

"Sorry, we're cash-only," I said.

"You're cash-only?"

"Yes."

"I don't have cash. Cancel the order."

"Your food is ready. How am I going to cancel the order?" I couldn't just wiggle my damn nose and turn her beef quesadilla back into a cow.

"Cancel the order," she repeated as she scurried for the door.

A few four and five-letter words later, I knew I didn't want to repeat that interaction. She wasn't the first. It had happened before, and it was bound to happen again.

We had to do something, and taking cards seemed like a no-brainer. Still annoyed over the beef quesadilla I had to eat, I asked Mom if she'd be willing to consider taking card payments, and to my surprise, this time, she said okay.

# One, Click, or Two

"It usually takes fifteen minutes for the drops to kick in," the nurse warned. "And things may look yellow, so don't worry if they do. It's totally normal." My head was already tilted back; she was positioned behind me. "Look up," she said. Her finger pressed down on my upper cheek to hold my eye open. *Drop.* "Other eye," she said as she pivoted to my left side. "Okay, look down, please." *Drop.* She went to the cabinet and put the drops away. "The doctor should be here shortly."

Across from my chair, I saw a sign with some verbiage about melanoma. To my right was a diagram of an eye. What a mysterious organ! Disgusting looking. Hard to believe that the quality of life depended on two little balls in my head.

I looked at my phone. The apps were blurry and barely identifiable. I looked up at the melanoma sign again. Only the capital letters were legible.

The doctor came in and extended his hand; his grip was appropriate. He asked how I was. I said, "well," careful not to say "good" in front of someone so educated. He rolled a contraption to my chair.

"We're going to go over a few images. Tell me which of the two is clearer."

I looked through the lens.

"One," click, "or two?"

"Two."

"One," click, "or two?"

"Two."

"One," click, "or two?"

I paused. He went over the images again. "One?" click, "or two?"

"One."

"One," click, "or two?"

I wanted to take my time. I paused again. Click. Click.

"Two."

When we finished with the right eye, we moved to the left and did the same thing.

Like most doctor visits, I spent a total of ten minutes with the doc himself. At the register, I looked out the door. Not so bright outside, not bad at all. I paid my bill and was handed a sheet of paper that was both my receipt and a prescription. I couldn't focus on a single character. Outside, the clouds had parted. "Oh my," I said, suddenly unable to see.

A basket on the counter was filled with complimentary disposable sunglasses. I grabbed a pair and covered my semi-functional eyes. On my way out, I reached for my phone. I'd taken an Uber to the doctor's office, knowing that driving back home with dilated eyes wasn't the best idea, but I thought I'd still be able to see my phone. The addresses I'd entered on the app were illegible. With my luck, I'd order an Uber and end up at the airport. I scanned recent calls for the letter that most resembled an L and called it, fingers crossed it was my brother Luis. No one answered.

I had no other option, so I walked home.

The most common item customers left at the café were glasses. We had to keep a lost-and-found bucket just for them. In my peppy years, during slots of boredom before or after dinner, I'd try on a pair, turn toward the kitchen, and look down the line. Sometimes, I'd make a goofy face, trying to draw a chuckle from one of the cocineros.

As the years passed, I began putting glasses on the ledge beside the register, hoping the owner would return. Usually, they did, but if they didn't, after a week or two, the glasses went into the bucket.

One afternoon, when I came in, I saw a pair of thin lenses held together by skinny wires. I tried them on for old times' sake, hoping I could crack a smile from the planchero. But as soon as they were on my nose, I noticed the trees across the street. The trees had transformed into individuals: individual branches, individual twigs, individual leaves. I couldn't believe it. When did my vision become blurry? I got the rise I was looking for, though not from the planchero, instead from the glasses themselves.

I took the wires off. The part that rested on the bridge of the nose was broken and dug into my skin. I put the wires back on the ledge. Surely, my new treasure still belonged to someone, their aid to a vivid world.

With all the sunglasses I'd collected over the years, I didn't think to bring a pair. The drops had made everything blurry, blinding. Crossing a bustling intersection was a challenge. I couldn't see the walk sign, so I moved parallel to the cars as they crossed the intersection.

Luis called.

"Hey!"

"You rang?"

"Yeah, I just left the eye doctor and can barely see ..."

"They dilated your eyes?"

"Yeah. I can't see well enough to get an Uber. It was a miracle I was able to call you. I was going to ask you for a ride, but I'm walking now. I just crossed 2222. I think I'll be fine."

"Gaaaa!" Luis mocked. "You know there's a machine that does all that now?"

"Really?"

"Gaaaa!" he mocked again. "Yeah, dilating the eyes is a thing of the past. But since your insurance sucks, you got outdated treatment. Gaaaa!" He asked if I was willing to pay a few thousand dollars for LASIK treatment. When I told him I'd rather wear glasses, he taunted me more in that brotherly I-love-you kind of way. "Alright, man, just be careful walking back," he said. "Let me know if anything happens."

After that first intersection, trekking was a breeze. Austin was my backyard. I knew my way around, muddled vision or not. I had mentally mapped all the major intersections. When crossing the highway, Hancock Drive was the most pedestrian-friendly. I knew which neighborhoods were quietest, which roads were sleepiest, and which parks I could cut through. My only concern was that within the first few minutes, my pinky toe started rubbing against the brown huaraches, which I hadn't worn in years.

There's an unspoken rule about how long to wait before claiming items left at the café. Boujee sunglasses: two weeks. A book: one month. A laptop: never. A phone: never. A sweater or jacket went to Goodwill or was given to someone caught unprepared during a cold snap. For the wire-rimmed glasses, one month seemed appropriate.

After a couple of weeks, I put them under the counter by the cash box to get them out of sight. A few days later, they went missing. The owner might have claimed them, but I had a feeling that Mom or Aunt Bobbie had tossed them in the trash, thinking the wires were too mangled for any owner to still love. I took their disappearance as a sign that my days of poaching from the lost-n-found were coming to an end. It was time to schedule an appointment with an optometrist and pony up for my own prescription.

I was only a few blocks from home with all the major boulevards crossed. I saw a couple crossing the street ahead of me. "Hey Julio," the man said. Both faces were out of focus.

"Hey there. I'm so sorry, but I just left the eye doctor. Who am I talking to?"

"It's Joe." Who's Joe? When I got closer, I recognized a long-time patron of the café.

"Oh, hey!"

"Have y'all met before?" He was referring to his friend. We looked at each other and shook hands.

"Did you just leave the optometrist?" she asked. Surely, the wonky sunglasses gave it away.

"Yeah, they just dilated my eyes."

"You know they have a machine that does that?"

"Really?"

"I think it costs a hundred dollars extra. Anyway, it's worth it. The last time I had my eyes dilated, I spent hours next door at a Taco Cabana waiting for them to focus. Where's your optometrist?"

"Off Balcones and 2222."

They were surprised I'd walked so far. "After a walk like that, I think you earned a snack," the friend said.

"You know, I live like two blocks that way," Joe said. "I can give you a ride."

"Thank you. I'm just a couple blocks away from home myself. I'll be fine."

Two bends later, I was home, sure my pinky toe needed to be stitched back onto my foot. I didn't bother opening the fridge, knowing all I had was butter and a bottle of Cholula. I could easily have walked to the store, I took my truck instead. I wasn't hungry, but after slogging for an hour and a half from the optometrist, I'd walked enough. And I'd earned a snack, dammit.

# Chicken Bones

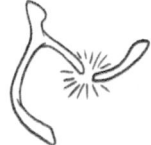

In a world of nuggets, tenders, and boneless wings, no one wanted to deal with chicken bones. Even dogs can't eat them. So, corporate meat packers had found a solution to the bones conundrum.

The restaurant depended on rotisserie chicken. What wasn't sold as quarters, halves, or whole chicken was used for enchiladas, tacos, chalupas, quesadillas, and nachos. We had very little waste, but we were still at war with the bones. We didn't have a high-speed deboning machine. The cooks did it by hand. Pulling chickens apart may seem like an unskilled job, but it has its challenges, bones, and bits that are easy to miss.

The legs have a sizeable femur-like bone and a smaller one, long and skinny and pointy at one end, the kind cartoon cats use to clean their fangs after raiding the birdcage. It's easy to miss while pulling the leg meat away from the more prominent bone. The bone highest on the breast, closest to the neck and head, is the wishbone. When we took the chickens from the rotisserie and cut them in half with heavy-duty shears, the wishbone snapped in two, and the pieces, now buried in the cleaved breasts, were especially easy to overlook.

When I bussed tables, an unmade wish often remained on the plate.

The gristle also has to be removed. The leg and thigh have more fat and unwanted bits than the breast and wings, which may be why dark meat has more flavor. One of the pieces most commonly missed is the slippery, stringy connective bit at the end of the leg, the chicken version of the quadricep or hamstring.

One evening, a cocinero made a taco while watching the Club América game on his portable TV and overlooked the leg bone. When the customer saw the giant bone in his taco, he called me aside and gave me an earful. He thought it had been intentionally left because he had come in just before closing. Embarrassed, I tried to assure him that wasn't the case. The planchero must have been distracted by the soccer match.

When I mentioned something to the planchero and told him to focus on work and not the soccer match, he got upset.

Papá often told the story of how he dealt with a customer who found a bone in his chalupa and was very verbal about it. Papá went to the kitchen, put a whole chicken on a plate, and brought it to the table. Then, he proceeded to pull the chicken apart, demonstrating how the bone had arrived on the customer's plate.

I didn't have the cojones to pull off that move. If a customer complained about a chicken bone, I'd ask, "Are you okay?" I think people respond better to that. If they're not okay, I ask, "Is there something I can do to make things right?" Thankfully, most of our customers are understanding. They just want me to know.

We've been at battle with chicken bones for decades. We can't afford an industrial deboning machine, and if we could, where would we put it? Bones give chicken flavor. What would our customers say if our food started to taste like nuggets and tenders?

# Tía Camamelo

Each of my mom's sisters did something unique that fit her personality. Lola gave us sweaty kisses after working in the yard. Norma sang lullabies when we spent the night. Norris was an exquisite cook and wore cool pants with patches. Susie was young and like one of us. Pat's watch had a stopwatch on it, which gave us structure. And one tía was always at the restaurant. We came to know her as Tía Camamelo.

No matter where she was— Christmas at Mamá Abuela's, or a primo's birthday, or even at the restaurant—whenever we saw our tía, we charged her with our hands extended, howling "¡Tía Camamelo!"

"Okay, okay," she'd say, reaching for her purse. Then she'd pull out a camamelo for each of us. There's no such thing as a camamelo. We meant to say caramelo – candy –but we hadn't mastered the pronunciation yet. It was like Halloween whenever we saw her, or so we believed. What we thought were candies were really Certs breath mints. Both were hard and sweet, the mints artificially so.

I'd ask Tía Camamelo if I could touch her hair. She usually said yes, though only if I didn't mess it up by pulling it forward. It was always combed back tight, not a hair out of place, como una mujer trabajadora, like a working woman. She probably used an entire can of hairspray or some kind of epoxy. Whatever it was, her hair was stiff. She could have ridden a motorcycle down MoPac at seventy miles an hour without a helmet and not displaced a single hair.

As we grew older, we quit asking Tía Camamelo if we could touch her hair or even if she had candy. We weren't cute toddlers anymore. We had a few years of schooling under our belts and knew about numbers, history, and how to enunciate words. I can't remember exactly when, but eventually, we quit calling her Tía Camamelo and started to call her Aunt Bobbie.

# Seis

"Happy Cinco de Mayo!" the customer exclaimed, excited to be in the café.

"Happy Cinco de Mayo to you, too." My reply was not nearly as bubbly. The holiday created pandemonium in the café, and at that moment, both rain and a rita-crazed crowd were in the forecast.

"How do y'all celebrate Cinco?" the customer asked.

"I usually have to work," I replied in an aguafiestas killjoy tone. "It's one of our busiest days of the year."

It was difficult to match the customer's enthusiasm when I was laser-focused. Cinco was the climax of the busy season, the ultimate test. If the chain of operations had a brittle link, Cinco was the day that link would be exposed, and the days leading up to Cinco were cortisol-filled as well.

After so many years of working on Cinco, call me a wet blanket, but when people say "Happy Cinco de Mayo," what do they mean? With so many holidays on the calendar, how can we remember what we're celebrating? May the Fourth, a Star Wars homage, is celebrated the day before. May the Fourth be with you. The day after Cinco was National Beverage Day. Then came the Kentucky Derby, and after that, Mother's Day. I'm not complaining. People love to go out and drink and spend money on those special days, which is good for business. That's why we celebrated Cinco de Mayo on Seis de Mayo, laughing all the way to the bank.

Our Seis de Mayo celebration came with its burden. I promise I'm not superstitious, but based on my experiences, Cinco de Mayo is a cursed holiday. In terms of flow and operation, we always have pickles on Cinco.

Typically, Cinco appeared in my periphery just after Valentine's Day. We needed a solid team from mid-March to the end of May for the busy season. But when the pandemic arrived, our sales shriveled to a fraction of normal. Our mornings and lunches were nonexistent. We kept a bare-bones crew to accommodate our bare-bones sales.

The global pandemic paused for three hours on Cinco de Mayo, and we got clobbered. People formed the most socially distanced line they could. The phone rang off the hook, and before long, we had so many orders it took more than an hour to get the food out, more than twice our longest wait time, even on the busiest days.

An unfortunate young couple who came in like chipper parakeets were almost in tears by the end of their wait.

"I'm so sorry," I told them. "We're getting absolutely slaughtered tonight. Can I get y'all anything to drink? To-go ritas, maybe?"

"Yes," the girl answered, shaking.

"Frozen, ok?"

"Yes."

The older I get, the younger young people look. With their masks on, they seemed on the cusp of the legal drinking age. I didn't have it in me to ask them for their IDs.

Years before, I'd fallen hard for a young lady, and a few days before Cinco de Mayo, she told me she'd come by the café with a friend. It was nice that she thought of me and wanted to visit, but a bit worrisome, as there was a good chance she would see me getting tossed like a rag doll.

That evening, there was a torrential downpour, and our roof leaked in several places, two or three of them in the dining room. The word "leak" doesn't do justice to the water that poured in. Mother nature opened a spigot, and cascades of water dumped onto the tables, booths, and floor. Our roof had leaked for years, but just a few manageable drops. That night, buckets weren't enough. We had to use bus bins. And between the hovering crowd waiting to be seated, the bus bins, saturated ceiling tiles on the verge of crumbling onto the floor, the embarrassment, and all the ambient noise, I missed noting that the friend my lady brought with her had requested corn tortillas instead of flour. When their food came out, I was promptly reminded. Flour tortillas are not the end of the world, but I was trying to make a good impression on my crush.

Now, it felt as though the ghost of that Cinco past was haunting me. Dark clouds rolled in, and the smell of moisture hit me every time the front door swung open. Please, not today, I pleaded silently with the ghost.

It was still early. People trickled in, placed their orders, called the rain's bluff, and went outside to wait, only to rush back in minutes later. Our awning was no match for a horizontal downpour.

It rained for fifteen minutes at most, then people slowly started to come in again. The green light came on when the clouds parted.

The kitchen redlined for nearly three hours, without so much as a moment for a sip of water. But the ghost didn't rear her head. The crowd was jovial and mature and everything in-between, not bothered by having to mop up the rain on their tables.

Toward the end of the rush, a dad wearing a red "Cinco de Drinko" T-shirt came in with his two sons. He studied the menu.

"You've been waiting all year to wear your shirt, huh?" I asked.

"Yeah," he said, grinning. "I love this shirt."

"Here's your table number."

"We can sit anywhere?"

"Anywhere you like, as long as we can see your number." His sons were already at the only free table.

I no longer care whether people know why they're celebrating. What difference does it make if the dad and his sons don't know about the conflict in Puebla between the French and the Mexicans? Maybe Cinco is the reason he held onto one of his favorite shirts, a reason to eat tacos with his sons. If you ask me, that's reason enough to celebrate.

# Shut Up and Stay

It was mid-afternoon when I inspected the front patio, looking for things that needed to be tidied. I prided myself on being a good right-hand man, though I doubted my ability to take on the challenge of an owner. I second-guessed my judgment all the time. For instance, the patio tables had been cleared, but they were covered with a thin layer of dirt deposited by the summer breeze. I debated whether they were worth a wet rag. Before I finished, the rag would be ruined, gray, and caked with filth. And for what? Only a handful of people sat outside during the pits of summer, half of them unwilling to wait for a table inside. An owner would never debate if a white rag was worth a few patrons. An owner would wipe all the tables without giving the white rag a second synapse.

One car was in our parking lot, and the lot across the street was empty, too. Out of nowhere, a voice called, "Julito!" Only a few people outside the family called me Julito. My friend came over, and we hugged.

"Sorry, I was taking up space in your lot, but I'm waiting for two other people."

She'd just returned from the California coast and said it was amazing. I asked her if she'd like a little something—a rita, chips and salsa ... She was fine with water.

A couple came in, took one step toward the seating area, then one step toward the register, and froze. I could tell they were new by the way they looked around with how-does-this-work written on their faces.

"Hey there. Here are the menus. We don't have a waitstaff on the floor. I'll take your order at the register when y'all're ready."

They didn't study the menu for long. The lady asked if the guisada meat was tender. I said it was and that the plate had recently become quite popular. She ordered the guisada and a Modelo beer. He ordered beef nachos and iced tea. They took the coolest four-top in the house, the one furthest from the front door.

The front door squeaked open. It was the second friend. "Julio!" she exclaimed and came in for a hug. I asked how she was. She told me they'd been in Michigan for the last two weeks and had just gotten back. The smoke from the wildfires had affected their trip. They hadn't been able to spend as much time outdoors as they'd planned.

While they waited for the third, the second friend ordered a Mexican martini for them to split, and guacamole and chips for the table.

It was time for the guisada and nachos to go out. Nachos always take longer than other plates, especially if you like that charred cheese texture on top. Shortly after their food went out, the lady called me to the table.

"Excuse me," she said. "Where are the potatoes? I ordered the guisada, and this isn't guisada. Guisada has potatoes. And this meat is tough." She poked it with her fork, like a kid prodding a possum with a twig.

"The guisada doesn't have potatoes."

"Yes, it does. Where I'm from, Houston, where there are *real* Mexicans, guisada has potatoes."

I'd dealt with expert critics before. No point in arguing with someone so familiar with Mexican food. I went along to an adjacent booth that needed to be bussed and kept working as if nothing had been said.

"Here," she said, lifting her guisada plate with both hands. "This isn't good, I'm not eating this."

"Okay," I said, again unwilling to engage with her. I took the plate to the back.

The staff looked puzzled. "¿Qué tiene?" Monse asked.

"No lleva papas," I replied, leaving her plate.

"Pero la guisada no lleva papas ..."

The table I'd just bussed needed to be wiped down, so I went over it with a wet rag. The lady didn't say anything to me as I walked by. If she doesn't want to eat, su pedo.

She got up and made her way to the front counter. I followed her. Whatever blood wasn't pumping to my legs pumped to my face. If anyone gets the venom, it's her.

"I've been eating guisada my whole life," she said, "and not once have I had it without potatoes."

My hands whizzed over the terminal in search of her order.

"Have you ever been to Houston? Do you *know* how many Mexicans live there?"

"It was the guisada and the beer, right?"

"Yes." I found her order and started the refund process.

"I'll have your money back here in one second. I'm not charging you for anything. You can have the beer."

"I'm not asking for a handout. I'm fine with a different plate."

"I think a refund is our best option," I replied. Anything to make her shut up. And how is another plate of food not a handout?

"But I need dinner ..." she said, her shield lowered. Then it sprang back up. "You know, whatever," she snapped. "I won't eat."

The softness in her voice hung in the air, the part about needing dinner. Despite her inflammatory comments about Houston and real Mexicans and Mom's guisada, she was hungry and needed dinner. I stopped the refund process, looked down at the counter, dug deep, and looked back up at the lady. The third friend walked in. I redirected my attention to the lady.

"You know, I've been doing this for a long time, and we succeed at this by getting people to come back. If you're not satisfied with your food, I'm more than happy to swap it out for something else. And I really do mean that." I paused to see if she was receptive. Our eyes met. "What can I bring you?"

"I would like the beef nachos."

"I'll bring the nachos to your table." I scribbled her order on the notepad, hung it in the queue, and returned to the register.

"Julio!" the third friend bursted out. "How are you doing?"

"I'm okay, and yourself?" It was the truth and a lie. I was delighted to see my friends, but still rattled by Miss Potato.

"I just got back from Germany."

"Oh yeah? How was that?"

"It was exactly what I wanted ..."

"Okay, Julio." The second friend said. "We're all here. I think we're ready to order."

"I don't know what I want," said the third, stepping behind the first two to study the menu.

The second friend insisted on covering the guacamole, ordered an entrée, split the Mexican martini with the first, and ordered a flan. The first always ordered chicken soup. The third ordered chicken tacos. When I asked if she wanted corn or flour tortillas, she insisted on corn. "Oh my God, Germans eat bread with everything! Seriously, if you go to Germany and don't eat bread, good luck."

No one was in line behind her, so I asked about her travels. Her trip was less a vacation and more a full immersion into the German language and culture. She'd wanted to experience everyday German things, like going to the grocery store and the doctor's office and ...

"Are you done ordering?" the second friend asked. "Sorry, but I'm starving."

I didn't charge my friends full price. I rarely did, which is another reason why I wouldn't be a good restaurant owner. I handed out food to make Miss Potato shut up and gave food to those I adored and wanted to stay.

# Kill Them with Kindness

Of all the things on this planet, the one thing I wasn't allowed to have was an enemy. At least not while I worked at the restaurant. We got paid for being agreeable and pleasing people. Even if the customer was snarky and unpleasant or claimed he was always right, I turned my cheek and moved on.

Mom had a favorite saying when it came to dealing with people. Boca cerrada no entra mosca – a fly can't enter a closed mouth or don't talk so much. I took what she said as true regarding sensitive topics like religion and politics. I rarely touch them and never in a way that reveals my hand.

I interacted with the public for so many years that it was inevitable I'd strike somebody the wrong way. We had a tool for that. Or I should say, Uncle Frank had his method. He advised us to kill them with kindness, which I assume he learned from decades of working at his bar on Sixth Street. If you're kind to everyone, you can't have an enemy, right?

Lord, how dull! Having no enemies is like eating totopos sin salsa. What kind of life is that? I have to have at least one enemy

I can point to. I try not to have any enemies, but having my feathers ruffled a little might spice up my life.

Choosing an enemy is a delicate matter, almost an art. Ideally, my enemy wouldn't be a pushover, but not vicious, either. If they write a blistering review, I'm fine with that. Mom and I don't read them. But I'm not so fine if they chuck a brick through our window or clog our toilet with wads of paper towels. The last thing I want is someone who salts our crops. Or worse, someone who would harm Mom or me or the family.

Come to think of it, fabricating an enemy isn't necessary. We already have them. Just go outside, and you'll see. They're sitting at the tables on the patio, on the bench, and on my car, and your car, too. Look up! They are on the power lines, waiting for you in the trees. That's right. I'm talking about those vexing grackles.

Most major cities have some kind of feathered foe. Beach towns, like Corpus Christi, have seagulls. And while I find them charming, I'm quite sure they're not, especially amongst restaurateurs with patios. New York City and London have pigeons. I once saw a sign that read, "Don't feed the pigeons; they're vermin." Those birds, with their beautiful iridescent feathers, were labeled rodents. Male grackles have iridescent black feathers and a blue-purple hue around their heads and chests. But those shiny feathers don't fool me.

There's no shortage of grackle sympathizers in Austin. Artists glorify them. The grackle's native habitat is a shopping center parking lot. Loitering comes naturally to the grackle, especially on power lines and in the trees. If you go grocery shopping on a scorching day, don't park in the shade of a tree to keep your car cool. Big mistake. Your pal, the grackle, has been watching and waiting, holding it in all afternoon for this very moment.

Bombs away on your sunroof and windshield. Bombs away on our patio tables, the Mexican martinis and enchiladas. Bombs away on your blouse, your hair. Grackles don't care. Hasn't happened to you yet? It's only a matter of time. I've been struck on my shoulder and shirt many times, even once on my nose.

From what I can tell, the grackle problem is getting worse. Grackles used to swoop down on people's plates after they'd left their table. Or, say you're sitting on the patio and go inside for a saltshaker. More than likely, when you returned, you'd find a grackle slip 'n slidin' in your caldo or leaving dinosaur footprints in your refried beans.

Grackles are evolving, but not in a good way. They're becoming more aggressive. I recently saw one dive onto a table while customers were still dining, snag a loose chip from the corner of the basket, and fly away. I even saw a grackle snatch a chip from a toddler's hand. The poor child nearly began to cry, and the parents were stunned. It takes something like that to make grackle sympathizers reconsider.

When Uncle Frank still worked at the café, he zip-tied spikes under the awning frame to keep the grackles from perching directly over the customers. We could have done more, though. Some businesses put up owl figures to spook them, the grackle version of a scarecrow. If you can afford it, you can buy an owl figure that makes owl sounds, even a Terminator owl whose eyes light up red as the owl sounds blast out.

The spikes Uncle Frank installed had a limited effect. Turns out, grackles can land anywhere, and covering every surface with spikes wasn't feasible. They'd just wait up high in the trees where we couldn't put spikes. The techno owl seemed perverse, worse than the problem itself. The best we could do was bus the tables as promptly as possible, preventing the grackles from making a mess on them and the floor while they feasted on leftovers. Some customers assisted us in our battle and bussed their tables.

Having an enemy is still new to me. A busser once told me he'd accidentally killed a grackle by rolling up his damp towel and popping it, locker room style. A flick of the wrist had been enough to kill the bird.

Part of having an enemy is gathering intel. When it was slow at work, I peered through the window and studied the grackles from afar. Some of them seemed famished and scraggly. A few were wiggling their feathers and crying in a unique way. Soon after, I watched a healthy grackle feed the malnourished grackles mouth to mouth. Then it dawned on me. The healthy grackle was the mother, and the scraggly grackles were her children. Or should I say teenaged grackles, not totally helpless but still dependent. They could fly and kind of knew what to do, but were still callow.

When I bussed the tables on the patio, all the adult grackles flew away if I got too close. Not the teenagers. They hadn't learned fear yet and continued to rummage even as I lifted the plates. I could have reached over and taught them what fear was about. Instead, I shooed them until they flew away.

Damn it. I was teaching the next generation of grackles to fear people less than the generation before. My enemy, the winged reptile, was getting more sympathy from me than I cared to give. My firm stance was becoming less rigid.

It was late spring, but it felt like the second month of summer, and hadn't rained in forever. When Mom brought a gun to work, I knew it was for the grackles. It didn't shoot bullets or BBs or pellets. She filled it with water.

We'd give the grackles a much-needed bath, a cooldown from the Texas heat. For whatever reason, the birds never stuck around for the bath. And after a couple of weeks, they began flying away at the mere sight of the Pavlovian toy.

In time, the heat would pass, and winter would arrive. Spraying them in winter would be cruel. In a few minutes, the water would turn frigid, and I didn't want the grackles to shiver and suffer. I'd get to the winter solution when the weather turns. Until then, bath time it was.

# Broken Printer

We'd just closed for the evening, and I finally had the peace I needed to change the old receipt printer. The printer wasn't vital to the operation, we could still text and email receipts. The real problem was that the cash drawer wouldn't open. A brilliant team of engineers somewhere insisted that the cash drawer connected to the sales system via the printer. This meant that if, for whatever reason, the printer went on vacation, the cash drawer automatically became its plus one.

A few days earlier, after an hour on the phone with tech support and another half hour with the manufacturer, we narrowed the problem down to a defunct cable, which I replaced. The printer and cash drawer worked for a day, then decided another vacation was in order.

I unboxed the new printer, connected it to the system, and tested it. Nada. I tried to open the cash drawer. Still nothing. The manufacturer's service hours ended at four in the afternoon, so it would have to wait until morning. I retreated to the warmth of my phone. My brother Luis had sent an attachment. He often sent me immature videos or memes. I could use a lift.

A new AI chatbot had just come out, and everyone claimed it was the beginning of the end. Luis had taken the time to tinker with it and sent me a screenshot of his conversation. His question: How would a skeptical, paranoid, and controlling restaurant owner go about finding a dependable and honest manager for the business?

I was flattered that he'd thought of us and assured myself he hadn't meant to insult me.

I immediately noticed that his question was redundant. He could have just said, "Restaurant owner." The AI bot would have known that all restaurant owners—at least the successful ones—are skeptical, paranoid, and controlling. As if those were negative traits! In the context of running and owning an eatery, they were essential attributes, the survival traits needed to endure and go the distance.

Before I could dig into the machine's response, the contrarian in me came up for a breath of air. I don't like machines, not the smart ones or the dumb ones. I didn't like VCRs when I used them, printers, or scanners. I don't like TVs anymore; the new ones have too many features.

With my skepticism on full alert, I read what the all-knowing machine had to say.

*1. Conduct a thorough background check.*

One worker cut his hair really short. The kids in school used to call it a bald fade. With his hair that short, you could see a scar that ran across the side of his head just above his right ear, wide as a permanent marker. When I asked him about it the first time, he responded, "Mira Julio, yo soy malo." If by bad, he meant badass, yes, absolutely. Hands down, he was one of the most reliable workers we had.

*2. Use a rigorous interview process.*

We once posted an ad for a dishwasher on the Facebook group La Chachara. I chatted with over a dozen people, only to have one person show up for the interview. After the third or fourth question, I asked her if she could stay and work that evening. We were between the sword and the wall and needed someone at that very moment.

She said yes, so I got her an apron, and she started on the spot. She's been with us for two years and counting.

3. *Use personality tests.*

Does this bot think I'm some kind of psychologist? The bot's answers and Luis's question burrowed deeper under my skin.

4. *Use trial periods.*

Interesting, maybe the bot is onto something.

5. *Trust but verify.*

The silly machine already forgot that successful restaurant owners are naturally mistrustful. Paranoia and skepticism are survival traits. Next!

Luis prompted the bot further: "What else could the restaurant owner do?"

The tireless machine went on: regular audits, surveillance cameras, clear policy and procedures, employee training, accountability systems. I was starting to feel incompetent. Despite nearly twenty years of experience, the machine thought it could do better than I could.

For years, I'd been thinking about how the machine takeover would play out. I was convinced that machines would push out drivers and physical workers first. Now they were knocking on my door. The line cook won't get the ax anytime soon, nor is there such a thing as a robo-planchero, or a cyborg lavatrastes. If anyone is kicked to the curb, it's me, the guy at the register, the guy who does the spreadsheet and clocks the hours. I'm the one who should be worried.

Not to bathe my tacos en crema, but I'm competent when remembering orders and names and the personal details people share with me. But I'm no match for the intelligence that stalks me. No one is.

Deep down, I know everything will pan out. When I was a kid, my tías used to say I gave the best hugs. Being chunky helped. I'll be damned if any machine will ever beat me at hugging. I'd put them on the menu under the margaritas: side hug $3, full hug $5, handshake complimentary with dinner and a drink. Free hugs will be a thing of the past, like free chips and salsa are a thing of the past.

"But I thought a hug came with the meal?" a customer might counter.

"My apologies," I'd respond, "Hugs are not priced in. They're a separate order."

Best not to preoccupy myself with super machines and my eventual redundancy. Who knows if it will ever happen? In the meantime, I have a dumb machine right here that doesn't work. I'll have to call tech support again in the morning. Surely, the human on the other end of the line will know how to get the printer going again.

# Chilaquiles

'm not a proud person. I'm really not. But as far as I am concerned, Mexican breakfast is untouchable. I struggle to find another cuisine that compares. And I'm not talking about breakfast tacos because they're their own thing. I'm talking about the traditional plates. Those dishes have marble columns for legs. For instance, huevos rancheros, ranch-style eggs, typically fried, with salsa roja drizzled over them. Huevos divorciados, like rancheros but with two different sauces, one per egg, hence the idea of marital friction. Or machacado, dry, shredded beef mixed with scrambled eggs, often with diced onion, tomato, and either fresh jalapeños or serranos. Without the carne seca, you've got Plain Jane Huevos a la Mexicana, which is still exciting. All those plates come with beans on the side and tortillas, too.

Before I get carried away, we can't overlook the king of Mexican breakfast, pound for pound, maybe the heaviest hitter on the Mexican breakfast circuit: los Chilaquiles - deep-fried tortilla, bathed but not soaked in salsa roja, a sprinkle of crumbled queso fresco and fresh onion—beans on the side and a fried egg or two on top.

There are a few interpretations of chilaquiles. Some people like to soak the fried tortilla for a long time for a softer bite. I personally prefer to preserve the chips' integrity and crunch. Some people serve crema on the side. I've also seen the option of adding bistec or chicken on top.

Like most dishes, there's a technique for eating chilaquiles. People who regularly enjoy Mexican food have their own method or order of operations. Tacos, quesadillas, and tortas each have their eating process, eating items with your hands is more straightforward. The sequence of steps for eating more complex dishes can be deeply personal. I have my method of eating chilaquiles.

The construction phase is first, meaning every bite must be individually constructed. The base of the bite requires a chilaquil foundation, and I build up from there. I skewer a small cut of fried egg on my fork, then a dollop of beans and a dot of either yolk or crema, though I strongly encourage both. That's one bite. The next bite is a mirror image of the first: chilaquil, then egg, then bean, then crema and or yolk.

The construction phase ends when the eggs, chilaquiles, and beans are eaten. The plate should look like a fancy abstract painting, a mixture of salsa roja, beans, yolk, and crema swimming on a colorful canvas. Next is the reverse artist or deconstruction phase. Chilaquiles are usually served with bread on the side. I use a bit of bread to unpaint the canvas. Dip the bread, let it soak, or swoosh it around on the canvas. Each pinch of bread is a reverse brush stroke, removing paint from the canvas. Unpaint the canvas until it's clean, like a plate that never touched food. If the eatery doesn't have bread to unpaint the dish, ask for a pair of tortillas. Tortillas won't sponge up the juices quite as well, but they'll do just fine.

New visitors sometimes asked if we served chilaquiles. We didn't. Some people have asked if we've considered adding them to the menu. Again, sorry. Not because the dish doesn't belong. We'd have to fry our own chips, which would be a pain since we didn't have a proper industrial fryer. Everything was fried by hand.

Otherwise, chilaquiles are easy. We'd use our ranchera sauce on top or salsa verde if that's what the customer wished.

Adding chilaquiles would also be dangerous. I like them too much. Hence, the self-imposed rule of only eating them when I travel south. In Mexico, I eat them pretty much every morning. When Austin was more accessible, I used to go to South Austin with Papá for chilaquiles. The place that served those marvelous chilaquiles recently opened directly across the street. At first, they were only open for late lunch and dinner. Later, they started opening in the morning, too, but only on the weekends.

That reminds me, when people asked if we served chilaquiles, and if we would ever add them to the menu, I always thought no. Our breakfast was excellent as it stood. Our migas, rancheros, and Mexicanas were champions—no need to add another piston to an engine that hummed beautifully. And the thought of serving something from our neighbor's menu made me feel funny, although there's nothing wrong with a bit of competition.

# Cigarette

Everyone had punched out for the evening, I pushed the front door to be sure it was locked, then pushed the sliding doors of all the refrigerators. They were closed, I pushed again anyway, just to be safe. If anything, checking the refrigerators was more important than checking the front door. The front has remained unlocked overnight many times before. Nothing happened. However, if one of the fridge doors got stuck overnight, all the food would be gone, and we'd be out five hundred bucks in parts and labor. I hit the lights, locked the back door, and rushed to the parking lot. The planchero always shared a cigarette with me, and I'd have to hurry if I wanted to bum a smoke. If no one stuck around to smoke with him, he might leave.

Vices need aphorisms for guiltless enjoyment. Alcohol has plenty of isms. In vino veritas is one of my favorites, so I modified it for smoking: lo cierto con un cigarro, the truth with a cigarette.

I saw the planchero's car in the lot, turned around, and went to the front patio. I could hear them there.

"... the owner was right there in the kitchen, asking the cook,

'¿Donde estamos?' And the cook turned to him and said, 'Look, you're in my way. Let me work and get out of my kitchen.'" Two people were listening, and a pack of cigarettes was on the table. I grabbed one and lit it.

"To the owner! He said that to the owner! 'Get out of my kitchen.'" The planchero took a pull of his cigarette. Three of us had cigarettes; the fourth had the apple he brought in his backpack every day. We took quiet pulls; he took loud crunches.

"Every Saturday, that spot gets three hundred tickets, all at least eight, ten tacos each. And each taco with three or four different ingredients: rajas, huevo, tocino, jamón, papa, chorizo. Can you imagine?" He took another pull. "Just one of those tickets would kill you. Imagine three hundred. Three hundred!"

"Who is this guy?"

"El bigotes. Of all my years working in kitchens, he is la máxima. He works at the Lamar location and makes, like, thirty-three bucks an hour. And he earns all of it. You think it gets busy here? Pssh." He threw his fist behind his head. "Ja! I would love to see tu tía work over there on Saturday morning, just one morning. Pobrecita! She wouldn't last half an hour."

It took me a while to understand the phrase tu tía. He called women he didn't like tu tía, your aunt. She could have been a grumbly customer, a tedious coworker, or really your aunt. If he didn't like her, she was tu tía.

"And what did the owner do?"

"He said, 'See you later,' and left. I couldn't believe it. The place gets three hundred tickets, ten tacos per order, and the owner just leaves?"

We took our final pulls. The story had been told, and only the cigarette filters remained. We said our goodbyes, went to our cars, and left.

One of the former cooks told a similar story. For many years, she'd worked at another Tex-Mex establishment where a guy did the kitchen all by himself: the salamander oven, the grill, the line, probably a fryer too—all of it, a two—or three-person job. Whenever someone tried to enter the kitchen, even the owner, he'd say the same thing, "Get out of my kitchen."

We didn't have a salamander oven or a fryer, so I didn't know what it took to operate that equipment. It seemed unlikely that one person could work all those pieces. And how could one guy pump out three hundred tickets with eight tacos per ticket and so many different ingredients?

I'm not calling the planchero a liar. I don't doubt there are shamans out there who can make it rain tacos. But I have a hard time believing, even with a cigarette, that Don Bigotes could hammer out that volume. Although, in a city that loves breakfast tacos so much, I wouldn't be surprised if one of these legendary shamans did exist.

# Break-In

Rarely, if ever, did I set my phone to airplane mode, not even
when I flew. I like to be reachable in case anything happens.
That night was different. My battery dipped below twenty
percent, and I wasn't near a charger. I'd just learned that setting the
phone on airplane mode saved juice.

The next morning, I woke up an hour later than usual, reached
for my phone, and noticed the tiny airplane icon next to the battery
icon. I'd forgotten the battery was low. As soon as I turned airplane
mode off, the phone buzzed. Aunt Bobbie had left a voice message:

"Okay, Julio, I tried calling your mom about twenty times. They
broke into the restaurant and took the cash that was back there.
Anyway, whenever y'all decide to call, and ... anyway. I don't know
what to do. Bye."

I phoned the restaurant, and Aunt Bobbie picked up. She was
calm and acted as if nothing had happened. I told her I'd be right
over. "Why? Everything's cleaned up, and the window guy is on his
way." There was no unusual commotion in the background, just the
hums and clicks of a typical kitchen. I jumped into my clothes and

beelined to the restaurant.

The front door window had been covered with a piece of cardboard. Aunt Bobbie was taking orders at the register. I asked everyone if they were okay, and they all said yes. Thankfully, the break-in had happened late at night when no one was around. We were doubly fortunate that the robbers chose to break the window on the front door. Of all the windows they could have crawled through, that was the easiest one to repair.

Everything seemed under control. The broken glass had been cleaned up; the cops had been notified, so I left. The window repair guy pulled in as I pulled out of the driveway.

When I returned for my afternoon shift a few hours later, there was zero evidence of a break-in. The afternoon crew came in shortly after I did, and I took pleasure in spreading the chisme. As one of the cocineras got to her station, I leaned toward her. "Did you know we were robbed last night?"

Her head snapped toward me. "Really? What happened?"

"They came in through the window and took the bag," I said, pointing to the newly repaired window.

She tilted over and glanced at the new window. "What else did they do?"

"That's it."

"Oh, okay," she said with fleeting attention and got to work. If another cocinero forgot to salt the beans, agárrate. But when I told her someone broke in overnight? Nada. What should have been a gushing stream of gossip was parched limestone, once a creek.

When I told the others in the back what happened, their responses were similar: They'd take a gander at the new window and then return to work. Fin. The burglars didn't take beer, liquor, meat, or the tablet we used for sales. They didn't tag the walls or vandalize the kitchen equipment.

Since going electronic, the cash we kept on hand was pennies compared to the piles we once had. Most of what the robbers took was in our change bag, disguised as a Husky tool bag. There were a few small bills, but the bag was bulky with quarters, nickels, pennies, and dimes. The real offense was that what should have been an exciting story was a snore. No one got a rise from the event, not even the police. I was told they wouldn't be there to investigate for another two weeks. A storyteller who doesn't get a reaction from his audience suffers just as much as a comedian who doesn't get a laugh.

I had to accept that the break-in had been a nonevent, but I continued sharing my story. A sizable portion of our customers lived in the neighborhood. I thought they'd like to know what happened. When I told one lady, she shared her own story. The lingering smell the burglar left in her house gave him away. She'd only been gone for twenty minutes, and boom, that's all it took. She rushed into her kitchen and was relieved that her French pots and pans were still there. The thief had made a bit of a mess looking for something, then left.

A gentleman I told pitched back his story of when a thief snagged his classic 1970s bike, an irreplaceable road racer. Unlike my story, his was a punch in the gut.

I empathized with the stolen bike because someone stole ours when we were kids. That didn't sit well with Mom. She drove everywhere in pursuit of what was rightfully ours, found the bike less than a mile away, and told the father of the kid who'd stolen it. He said the kid had traded our bike for a VCR, which turned out to be a lie. The bike returned home soon after.

The second time our bike was stolen, Mom went into momma bear mode again. She yanked me into the passenger seat and wove in and out of every street like yarn through a loom until we spotted the bike in someone's garage. Two or three stereotypical cholos in white tanks and baggy Dickies saw us cruising and snatched the bike out of sight, but they were too late. Mom darted out of the car like a Doberman and chewed them out. I have no clue what she said, but she stomped her foot when she said it. Again, the bike returned home.

The bike stories were memorable. Bicycles are often recognized as a child's first taste of freedom. Mom was the hero. The thief was the bad guy, and more importantly, he was identified. Both the problem and resolution were universal.

The café break-in lacked those things. Who was the protagonist? There was an antagonist, the thieves. But they were unidentified, leaving the audience with an unquenched thirst. The only evidence of the break-in was a broken window, which had been repaired by an uncharacteristically prompt repairman. The stakes were low to non-existent. A bag of small bills and quarters was peanuts to us, and for the thief, probably no more than a handful of visits to a washateria.

I'm not complaining about what happened. If the best crime story I had to tell was about shattered glass and a snatched change bag, I'd take it. Having a banger of a tale would have been much worse, and frankly, it wouldn't have been worth it.

# Cuaderno

It's been happening for years, the clash between labor and capital. It didn't begin with Marx or come to a head in the twentieth century when half of Europe was divided by ideology. The skirmish between labor and capital is eternal, and a world without it is unfathomable.

Even coffee shops and warehouses are unionizing. I don't have the slightest idea how unions are formed, but I know why: for power and a fair piece of the pie. We had a union at the café, quite possibly the oldest union of them all.

When Sara started with us, one of the veterans gave her the treatment. "Aquí no hay hojas sueltas, puro de cuaderno." There are no loose sheets of paper here, only the notebook. She'd said it in a like-it-or-not way. Here, you're one of us, period. There was no discussion. Sara didn't push back. She put her head down and worked silently. Many years later, she told me what happened.

The idea of the cuaderno is that if you yank one sheet, three sheets come out. You mess with one, you mess with the whole. That's how the union worked. Cuadernos come in more than one form.

Those bound by friendship are resilient, but real cuadernos ride or die until the bitter end. They're bound by blood, la familia.

Sara started at the restaurant as a lavatrastes and worked her way up over the years, earning trust. She had the morning shift. If we were short and needed to hire an extra worker, word first rotated within the café, and if the position wasn't filled, it was listed in the local Latino newspaper, *El Mundo*. One day, when we were short in the evening, Sara told her brother. Soon after the first brother came the second, for a total of three siblings working at the café. The ad never reached the paper.

At the time, I had no idea that three members of the same cuaderno were a lot. At a restaurant as small as the café, their clique amounted to more than twenty percent of the total workforce. If you messed with one of them, you messed with all of them. Nothing was ever verbalized, but that's how these things worked. If they ever decided to throw their weight around, the damage would be like a wrecking ball.

Nothing major ever happened, which isn't to say nothing happened. One of our evening plancheros had another job in the mornings. He'd had it for years, easily more than a decade. Three or four of them worked there, a solid cuaderno for the size of the taquería. I randomly asked the planchero how work was going at his other job. To my surprise, he confessed that he no longer worked there.

One day, a chef from a sister restaurant rolled up, and they started to talk about salsa. I don't know what was said or how, but within minutes, the conversation got so spicy that two or three of the four workers put their aprons down and walked out in unison—a cuaderno.

These unions are sometimes formed in unethical ways. Let's say two cocineros don't get along. One of them doesn't scrub la plancha properly. The other one makes a fuss to the manager. "¡No manches! I'm not complaining, but does the plancha look clean to you? Next time he's on the plancha, notice, you'll see." Such drama over a benign scuff. Or it could be a pan with a speck of soot on the bottom or a restroom that doesn't smell like Fabuloso or a spoon that doesn't shine – anything. Sometimes, but not always, these re-marks are motivated by hidden forces. It's not a coincidence that the cocinero complaining about his coworker also has a primo or cuñado who needs a job.

Say you're gullible like me. You took the bait, and now it's the cocinero and his cuñado. You mess up further. The cuñado has a primo, and you hire him. You haven't totally screwed up yet. These guys kick ass, work fast, and never complain. They're not perfect. They horse around. But for the most part, they're a pleasure to work with, and they knock out whatever you throw at them. Among them, they know a little about everything.

You get hooked by how hard they work, addicted to the point of over-dependence. That is made painfully clear when one of them begins to act out. For fear of retaliation from the cuaderno, you keep quiet and endure. The best way to move forward without rippling the waters isn't by direct contact. Going toe to toe would be too much. Instead, your best move is to hire the older woman's daughter, who needs work, too. The first cuaderno will compete with the second. At the very least, their attention will be directed away from you.

Before anyone calls me a union-busting capitalist pig, please give me one last moment. For the record, let it be known that I'm not pro hojas sueltas nor a pro de cuaderno guy, just like a rocket scientist isn't pro-gravity or anti-gravity. These are universal strategies used to maintain continuity in the restaurant. I belong to a cuaderno my-self. The founding members are Papá and Mamá Abuela, with Aunt Bobbie recruited as first lieutenant and later as co-owner. Many tías have come and gone. Uncle Frank worked at the café for a handful of years. Uncle Joel served time there before he joined the Navy. Two or three cousins have been involved. Marisa worked at the café for a couple of years. And Luis, too, though only for one day. Mom and I have been the foundation for the greater part of the last two decades.

We allowed other unions to form and wanted others to form cliques and bond. Even our own cuaderno needs to be checked now and then.

# Fast

No one was at the counter and plenty of tables needed to be bussed. I hurried to tidy the dining area before the next wave of customers arrived. I couldn't be bothered with the bus bin and made multiple trips: grab, stack, drop off, wipe, repeat. As I dropped off the stacks and spires of dishes, the lavatrastes looked up, "No por Dios, Julio, ¡eres muy fast!" It's fun to play with words and sprinkle English into Spanish. We did that often.

Damn straight, I'm fast. I just bussed all the tables in two seconds. "Gracias," I replied.

"Sí, Julio, eres muy muy fast..." the lavatrastes repeated, "... muy fastidioso."

The kitchen exploded in laughter.

As a general rule, if a word in Spanish sounds like a word in English, more than likely, it's that word. I thought the dishwasher had called me fastidious.

"Sí, Julio, muy muy fast," the lavatrastes repeated, laughing again. It was apparent I didn't know what fastidioso meant. After finishing the dining area, I went to the other side of the kitchen and asked the cocinera what fastidioso meant. The lavatrastes wasn't calling me meticulous. She was calling me annoying.

Such was learning Spanish in a kitchen.

# Are You Okay? Are You Okay?

For over a decade, I worked every Friday evening, which isn't as bad as it sounds. The rush and movement and regulars and crew made Friday nights a thrill. A few years ago, I was bumped down to Friday mornings and lunch. The schedule change meant a demotion in pay but a promotion in work-life balance. I could be on the other end of Friday afternoon happy hour.

It took me a couple of years to form a solid happy hour crew. One night, I randomly bumped into friends while eating wings and drinking tequila at a restaurant. They told me they were there every Friday for ritas. So, I went there again the following Friday, and that was the start of my new happy hour crew.

Our conversations ricocheted everywhere. We discussed politics, which I rarely did. When it was American politics, I spoke up; when it was Mexican, I listened. Austin came up in our conversations, as did where they were from –Guadalajara. One of my friends worked in a restaurant, so we talked about food and the process of serving and producing it. We spoke mainly in Spanish, sometimes bouncing to English. My friends were fluent in both eloquent Spanish and

Mexican vernacular, which was an advantage for me because my Spanish benefited from a non-kitchen environment.

The friend who worked in a restaurant always had a story. Most patios in the city were dog-friendly. As he was serving customers one day, their furry friend came out from under the table and bit his knee. The story was petrifying. I'm not much of a dog person. As a kid, I was terrified of dogs, and to this day, I still harbor residual fear. The dog's breed was— you guessed it—a pit bull. I asked my friend if he was okay and if anything could be done.

"No, no," he said. "I'm okay. The dog didn't want to hurt me because he could have. It was mild. It broke the skin, but really, the bite wasn't bad. The owner, however, held his phone up to my face, repeating, 'are you okay, are you okay, are you okay?' It was so bizarre, as if he was trying to record me saying I'm okay."

"The customer did that so he wouldn't get sued?"

"I guess. He didn't call an ambulance or try to get help. He just held his phone in my face and recorded me." He showed me a photo of the bite and assured me it wasn't as bad as it looked. No one was called. No charges were pressed. I was upset and thought he was too generous. My friend, a dog owner himself, had a lenient attitude toward the dog and the owner. Why should the dog pay the ultimate price for an ignoramus?

A few weeks passed, and I was serving happy hour again. An older gentleman had just begun making our patio his afternoon hangout. His face was a staple in the neighborhood. I'd seen him for years, decades even. He always wore heavy boots, his gait half tempo, exhausted.

He showed up alone or with one of his animals, which included a giant orange lizard, a bearded dragon, or a small, pug-snouted dog the crew called Chato, the flat nose.

He came by regularly enough for me to get a feel for each of his animals. Chato was harmless and stayed under the table. The lizard hissed at me once for stepping in his sunlight, which I suppose is what lizards do. He had a bigger dog, a tan, athletic husky-shepherd mix, massive enough to confuse with a dire wolf. He was always on a short leash, and for good reason. The first time I brought a rita to their table, the dog lunged at me. The bark he let out was as visual as it was audible, canines bared.

That's all it took. Just one lunge and I was afraid of the wolf-dog. I became hyper-aware and studied it through the window as they sat on the patio. The dog happened to yawn, and his jaw unhinged like a snake that swallows mice whole. His open mouth looked like a spiked boomerang. I heard that German shepherds are always aware of their surroundings. This dog was beyond aware. He was paranoid. Even when he yawned, he looked anxious.

Every time I delivered ritas to their table, I made sure there was tension on the dog's leash. The dog lunged again, and the owner yanked back on his leash, gripped him by his muzzle, and subdued him. The dog talked a ton after being subdued. I've heard that huskies like to talk.

Many happy hours later, after being subdued numerous times, the dog stopped lunging when I brought out a rita. He became more comfortable on the patio, and to a certain extent, I did, too. But I still looked for tension on the leash whenever I went to their table.

One afternoon, after the man had been coming in a few times a week for several months, he didn't go inside to order like the other customers but grabbed a seat at the corner table outside. I looked over at him, and he nodded as if to say, "One, please, rocks, no salt, no straw." We were all busy, including the barman, so I mixed the drink myself and hurried the length of the patio. As I placed the rita on the table, I caught a swift, silent blur from the corner of my eye and felt something on my right thigh. Wolfy had bitten me.

"No!" The man shouted, yanking the dog's leash. "No!" He did something to the dog's head to make it yowl, forcing it into submission on the floor, belly down.

"I'm so sorry. Did he break skin?" The man asked. I looked down at my leg.

"No, he got my shorts."

"If he broke skin, you just need water and Neosporin."

"He didn't break skin. He got me right here." I pointed to my shorts. "I'm good, really." I looked down and saw that the dog had tagged me, slobber in the shape of a bite.

"I am so sorry," the man repeated. "He did that to the mechanic the other day. In the same spot, too. He ain't trying to hurt nobody. He's just playing."

If the dog had already done this once, what would happen the next time? Every time I saw the man, he was with this dog and only this dog, just one playful nibble away from total isolation.

There was no evidence of a dog bite, not even a severed thread— like it had never happened. I told the crew about the bite and pointed to my shorts, where the dog drool would have been. The barman said he was uncomfortable taking drinks out to the man while Wolfy was around. Another cocinera refused to bring food to his table. She wasn't a fan of the way his lizard hissed at her.

I shared the story with my happy hour friends. If anything, I played the yarn down. It was barely worth sharing. There was no blood in my story, no ruined clothes, and certainly no buffoon with a phone in my face trying to record me saying "I'm okay."

# A Temporary Fix

"¡**N**o lo toques!" the cocinera barked.

I snatched my hand away.

"Leave it alone. I don't know if it will start again."

The day before, the rotisserie stopped working. When I hit the switch that spun the chickens, the motor didn't turn on. It just hummed. I flipped the switch again and again, praying for a different outcome. Soon, the motor didn't even hum. *Chin!*

Roasted chicken was the focal point of the restaurant. Half the menu depended on it. Customers who craved chicken needed the machine to work. No rotisserie meant no chicken; no chicken meant no job. Getting it up and running was beyond urgent.

The planchero pointed out a cog that was worn smooth as old cow teeth. Maybe that was the problem. I rarely serviced the rotisserie. It was always someone else. If it wasn't Uncle Frank, it was Papá or the tech or the planchero. We'd been using that machine for nearly forty years now. After all those years, the bulky, fire-breathing box was mostly a mystery to me.

We once had to replace the switch that toggles the motor on and off with a repurposed light switch. It worked so well that when it finally failed, I purchased another one at the hardware store. A thunderous pop and a few adjustments later, the rotisserie was working again. But I didn't have a drill, so I duct-taped the switch to the machine. My work was amateur and ugly as hell, but I reassured myself that it would do for the time being.

There was zero chance the hardware store carried rotisserie cogs, so I called Mom and asked where she purchased parts. She told me to call Papá. He said the company he used had gone out of business. I'd have to look elsewhere. Within half an hour, I'd sourced the cog online, but this time, I wouldn't be able to repair the machine with duct tape. Special tools were needed, tools I didn't have. I called our tech.

For the longest time, I thought his name was Don Ramón, because that's what the planchero called him. Supposedly, he looked like a beloved character from the Mexican TV show *El Chavo de Ocho*. Whenever we had a problem with kitchen equipment, we called El Don. Ice machine, refrigerator, freezer, you name it, El Don could fix it. When I called about the rotisserie, he knew how to fix that, too. Sunday at two-thirty worked for both of us.

Within a few minutes, we had the main shaft removed. The gear puller he used was surprisingly similar to the crank puller I'd used many times to remove bicycle cranks, but mine had a guide that made using it easier. El Don said his tool once had a guide, too, but it had worn down over the years.

The amount of caked grease on the shaft was embarrassing. We rarely cleaned that area, which wasn't so bad either. Once the cog was removed, it was easy to see that the new one should go on the cleanest section of the shaft.

As we remounted the shaft to the rotisserie, El Don glanced at the switch and paused. He was looking at the duct tape; my temporary fix turned permanent. I tried to explain myself. He chuckled. The problem with duct tape isn't that it looks terrible but that it works too well.

The moment of truth had arrived. We hit the switch. Nada. The motor still hummed, but nothing moved.

"Maybe the cog on the shaft is too snug to the gear on the motor," El Don said. "Go ahead and loosen everything up, and let's see if we can reposition it." I repositioned the shaft, and we toggled the motor on again. The cog barely moved. "It's not the cog," El Don said. "It's the motor." He spun the gear with his thumb and index finger, and the motor jolted into motion, spinning normally. "These motors have two speeds," he explained, "one to start the motor and the other to keep it going. The motor has problems getting going." He named the exact part of the failed motor—one of those names you instantly forget.

"This isn't a big deal. There's a place on Airport past 38th that sells these things," he pointed his finger at the motor. "It's been there forever. Forgot the name, though. It starts with an H. Anyway, they're not very expensive." He tinkered with the switch, spinning the gear by hand. "See how it spins both ways, sometimes clockwise and other times counterclockwise? That indicates that the first speed isn't working as it should."

He dove into the mechanics of the motor and explained how each gear was connected. I was interested and asked questions. Every question I asked had two answers. After three questions, I thought I knew everything there was to know about the rotisserie. At the very least, I'd learned that the auger-looking gear was called the worm gear.

For the time being, things were fine. I told our cocineros we'd have to spin start the motor by hand every time we used it and that it would eventually need to be replaced. Within a couple of weeks, El Don sourced the motor, and we scheduled a time to install it one evening after the dinner rush. As we worked, he told me that the broken motor probably wasn't original to the machine. It was probably a replacement, installed years before.

A few days later, I noticed a new light switch on the rotisserie. El Don must have changed the taped switch when I wasn't looking.

The switch still worked, but the duct tape had started to peel. He'd installed the new one properly with metal screws.

Every fix is temporary. In a few years, the motor will need to be replaced, and the repurposed light switch will break again. The gears will be worn smooth as bovine molars. And one day, our forty-year-old rotisserie will have had enough. Nothing lasts forever.

# Sustainable Models for Familial Enterprise

Friends and professors have approached me about applying for an MBA. One buddy went into the CPG world—consumer packaged goods—another dove into marketing. A guy from the gym went into analytics. The list goes on with all sorts of programs and specializations.

Whenever I think about applying for an MBA, I talk myself out of it because of the cost and time commitment. And considering how many years I've been at the café, I feel like I already have an MBA. My expertise isn't in restaurants or hospitality but in family business. After decades in the game, I think I understand the topic well enough to design a curriculum.

The familial business curriculum wouldn't differ much from other programs, but the required courses would include Sustainable Models for Familial Enterprise. The course would be a breeze, and the main principle would be simple: the proprietor of the business must name his first-born after the business. You don't have to name the business after yourself. Although it's advantageous, it's optional.

What isn't optional, however, is that your first child and the business *must* share the same name.

Let's say you sell pupusas or gorditas, and your name is José. You name your business Gorditas José. You work sixty hours a week, and your eatery finds success early and generates a regular following. After a few years, you and your wife are optimistic about life and decide to grow the family. Y'all have a kid. If you have a boy, you obviously name him José. If you have a girl, you name her Josefina. This is where it gets tricky because José and Josefina are not the same name. You might get away with keeping the name of the restaurant Gorditas José, but it would be better if you called it Gorditas Josefina. No need to approach the comptroller or Secretary of State or hire a lawyer to legally change the name. Changing the sign and menu to read Gorditas Josefina should work just fine.

I realize that this may sound ridiculous, but hear me out. We all know that the ego is powerful. That's why it must be harnessed to your advantage. If your first-born has the same name as the business, when the child grows up and the business needs a hand, you will be able to throw the child in, no problem. Your child will work like an ox. They'll have pride of ownership and attach a visceral feeling of self-preservation to the business.

Papá was a master of this principle. He could have authored the textbook for the Sustainable Models for Familial Enterprise course. His strategy was straightforward, but reinforcing the idea with an example wouldn't hurt. Graduate courses almost always use examples to illustrate the concepts being taught.

CASE STUDY ONE

Mr. Lucero was in real estate. Over the years, he noticed that the once-sizzling market was depleted of inventory. There were a lot more buyers than realtors and houses for sale. So, he had to get creative. By the grace of a greater good, Mr. Lucero found a twenty-acre lot half an hour outside town. His plan: subdivide the twenty acres into smaller lots and sell each lot separately. There were a few problems, however. The lot ran several acres deep, away from the main road. He'd have to build a water line and a road through the middle of the subdivision. Building a road is not as intuitive as it sounds. A project of that stature requires a skill set best satisfied by a civil engineer. There was a silver lining, though. He'd have the privilege of naming the road.

QUESTION ONE:

What should Mr. Lucero name his road?

ANSWER:

Mr. Lucero should name the road after his first-born.

QUESTION TWO:

Mr. Lucero was once in the hospitality business and named his first-born after his restaurant. What should Mr. Lucero name the road?

ANSWER:

If and when the first-born's name is already in use, the second-born's name will suffice. The road should be named after Marisa, his second child. If, for whatever reason, the project hits a snag, Mr. Lucero can count on his second child to step in and bail it out.

Which is precisely what happened.

When the project was nearly complete, Mr. Lucero was informed that one or two of his lots would have to be set aside and converted into a detention pond. He intuitively knew that a detention pond didn't make much sense. Rerouting the stormwater to a creek just behind the property seemed like a more straightforward, less expensive solution.

The engineer and Mr. Lucero's conversation about the two options soon turned into a dispute. Something didn't seem right. Whether you call it a coincidence or a calculation, Mr. Lucero's second-born child, Marisa, stepped in to help. She was in Houston, training to be a civil engineer then. Mr. Lucero drove to her house and laid the plans on her kitchen table.

The trip was fruitful. She saw that rerouting the drain water to the nearby creek was viable. Construction of the detention pond was averted, and the two lots were sold for full price. These are the sorts of things a child will do when a business or project is named after them.

These days, Papá is slowing down. All he talks about is going to the beach and doing nothing. He still has one eye on real estate, but forming another business or project might be beyond him now, which is good for his third child, Luis, who won't have to defend his ego like his two older siblings.

On second thought, having witnessed Papá's mastery of familial enterprise, I wouldn't celebrate yet. Let this be a warning to you, Luis. You are a credentialed nurse practitioner, and Papá is getting older. He loves nothing more than smoking his puro on the beach, which can be detrimental to his lungs. If something were to happen, heaven forbid, and Papá developed problems, do not let him name his lungs after you. More importantly, don't let Papá attach your sense of self to his lungs. That bond is nearly impossible to break. Trust me. Ask Marisa, too. We've been there, we know.

# Patada

We agreed that I would bring the hueso anillo, and she would get the chile guajillo. In hindsight, it was a bit lop-sided. The price discrepancy hadn't been on my radar. Obviously, meat costs more than dried chiles. The difference didn't bother me. I didn't know how to cook caldo de res. Monserrat did. She'd do all the work at first, but I told myself I'd eventually make it on my own.

Hueso anillo, bone ring, is the cut of meat typically used to make beef soup. In plain English, the cut is known as the shank. For those who prefer Italian, it's ossobuco. It was hard to gauge how much caldo we would eat. One anillo per person seemed about right, plus a couple more, assuming someone might help themselves to another serving.

First, the meat had to be soaked in tepid water, which didn't seem like a crucial step, but what did I know? Maybe it was one of those things Monserrat learned from her abuela.

After twenty minutes, I understood why she insisted on the soaking step. The meat water was murky, and whatever the anillos released, we didn't want to deal with it later.

While the meat water simmered, we prepared the vegetables, more or less the same ingredients we used for the café's caldo de pollo—zucchini, yellow squash, carrots chopped longways, chunky wedges of cabbage, and sliced celery.

"¿Elote?" Monse asked.

"Ehh," I uttered indifferently, which she took as a no.

"¿Papa?"

"¡No papa!" I was on the fence about corn, but I was sure I didn't want potatoes in the soup. She was sympathetic. Soup with potatoes invariably turns into potato soup. Potatoes are how kitchens turn a profit, especially with soup. While we didn't add potatoes to the soup served at the café, our caldo was sometimes bulked up with squash. As a filler, squash is infinitely better than potatoes.

The shanks cooked for around two hours. After the evening rush, Monse dry-toasted the guajillos on the plancha, then put them in the blender with water and salt and maybe a couple of chiles de arbol. She mashed the pulp against the strainer with a gloveless hand as if every drop of salsa was a nugget of gold. Monse looked over as I watched.

"You should wear gloves if you do this," she flexed. "You don't want to burn your hands." After decades of kitchen performance, her hands were immune to burns from chiles or flames—like the hands of a working woman.

At nine that evening, I flipped the open sign to closed, and we served ourselves. The guajillos turned the caldo red, like menudo. Few foods make the back of my neck tingle. After the first bowl, I helped myself to half a second. Even when I was full, I wanted more tingle. I said, "We should make caldo more often." Monserrat agreed.

The next time we made caldo de res, we soaked and cooked the meat, made the salsa guajillo, prepped the veggies, and added elote. I'd been iffy on adding corn, but the others were quite keen.

Again, the caldo was pure bliss. Picking around the elote wasn't a hassle. The only problem was that everyone fished for a beef ring, hoping to bag a piece of tuétano, bone marrow. Often, as the meat cooked, the marrow separated from the bone and swam in the abyss of goodness. Even if the caldo gods smiled and bestowed a button of marrow on you, one wasn't enough.

Monse was aware of our dilemma. A few soup batches later, she talked to her carnicero and brought a bag of big, honkin' marrow-filled bones, enough for everyone who wanted more than a morsel. Some spread the marrow on a corn tortilla, like butter on bread, and ate it that way. I thought mixing marrow with other flavors was criminal. I took the handle end of my spoon and ate it like bone pudding.

Sometimes, we were too lazy to buy elote from the store across the street. Sometimes, we forgot the guajillos and the caldo was clear instead of crimson. The others received the flavor changes well. "De donde yo soy, menudo is red, *not* caldo de res," one person stated with quiet authority. Where I come from, menudo is red, caldo isn't. Such a comment could spark trench combat. If you ask me, both versions have their place. Sometimes, I forgot to go to the carnicería before work, but otherwise, caldo de res became a Monday ritual.

Monserrat asked me if I'd ever heard of chayote. I hadn't. "It's like squash but different," she said. "I like to add chayote to the caldo when I make it at home." The lavatrastes overheard us and said she loved it, too. After we added chayote, someone mentioned epazote. I'd never heard of that, either. They told me epazote is an herb they used in caldo. The following Monday, with just one bundle of herbs, the caldo transcended the spacetime dimension. And the next week, although I'd mistaken hierbabuena for epazote, the caldo was still phenomenal. Every extra ingredient we added was another victory tallied to our winning streak.

One day, while buying the hueso anillo, I saw pata, cow's foot, on display. I knew what pata was used for but was too timid to experiment. When I asked the others if pata would be a good fit for our Monday ritual, Isabel became animated. Her cheeks lifted nearly to her ears. That was all I needed.

When it came to making the caldo every week, "we" is a large word. Nearly everything was done by Monserrat and sometimes another prep cook, often Isabel. The pata was not soaked in water like the shanks, nor was it cooked in the same pot. If the shanks took two hours to cook, the pata took at least three. By the end of it, the pata water was yellow, and the pata itself was translucent and wiggly. Everything about the pata, smell included, was enough to suppress the appetite of most eaters.

In the same way that the epazote added complexity to the caldo, so did the pata. It gave our soup an extra kick, a flavor, and a mouthfeel I hadn't experienced before. Priorities shifted. A couple of the guys fished out only pata when they served themselves. A guy who never ate our soup gave it a try, though he only slurped the broth.

What we didn't devour that night was stowed in a bucket. The true benefit of adding pata to the caldo became apparent the next day. The leftover broth was not liquid but a massive block of meat-vegetable Jello. The gelatin from the pata had turned the bucket of soup solid.

The following week, when I bought stacks of shanks, I also bought pounds of pata. For many weeks, on Tuesday mornings, I noticed the bucket of leftover caldo was just a little fuller than it had been the week before. One Tuesday, there were two buckets instead of half of one. The caldo's popularity had more than plateaued; it was in free fall.

On Wednesday, I noticed that the only dent made on the bucket was from the bowl I'd served myself the day before. I served myself another bowl. Three days in a row now. Just the smell of the soup made me wince. Never have I reacted to food that way. I ignored the kick and powered through until I put my spoon down and stared at what was left, a jiggly foot bathing in its juices.

I tossed the remainder in the trash. Days later, no one had made a pass at the bucket. The remainder of the salty Jello went in the garbage.

My romance with the caldo ended like most romances, with unchecked gluttony. We were done with soup. Adding feet once or twice was fine. But batch after batch, the flavor of the feet overpowered all the other ingredients.

One day, half a year later, someone mentioned caldo de res out of nowhere. Enough time had passed for the heart to miss what had once been fond. A few of us pepped up to the idea, including me. Cabbage, carrots, and squash went in without question, probably elote, too. I can't recall if we added chayote and epazote or hierba-buena. We wanted to keep the soup simple. This time around, we nixed the pata.

# There are Many Birds

The prep handed me two dollars. Usually, it was one dollar, but this time it was two. He passed them to me at waist level, his fingers discretely folded over the bills. I looked at his hand, then at his face. He nodded and winked his eye as if to say ya sabes. The lavatrastes a few feet away didn't see the handoff. La niña was prepping right there but didn't notice anything. Perhaps they were all intentionally oblivious to our interaction.

"Hay muchos pájaros en el tendedero," he whispered in a twelve-inch voice. I understood the pájaros part – there are many birds. The other word, tendedero, I hadn't learned yet. But I understood the message he was getting across. Don't let the birds see you. Don't get caught by the cocineras or your tía at the counter. They're loyal to Mom. If they see us, they'll chirp.

We'd done this many times before. The prep gave me a dollar, and I'd grab him a beer. He drank Dos Equis at first but later switched to Corona and, soon after, to Modelo Especial. After we closed and everyone sat at one of the booths and ate, a couple of the guys had a beer. Then, one evening, thirty minutes before closing, the prep asked if he could have his beer before dinner. We hadn't had a new customer in at least fifteen minutes, and only two or three tables were still occupied, so I said yes.

Half an hour before closing became an hour before, and it stayed there for a while. One day, just an hour after he showed up for work, the prep snuck up to the front counter and asked me for a beer. "Don't tell anyone," he whispered. "I was out until five in the morning. I didn't sleep well. Please, I need a beer. No más una," Just one, the hair of the dog, and that's it. "Put the beer in a to-go cup so no one will know."

I couldn't send him home. We were in a pinch, and he was all I had. He could have called in sick, but he didn't. What's one beer? He never missed work. Even if he could only operate at half speed, his fifty percent equaled somebody else's one hundred. I poured a beer into a to-go coffee cup and walked it over to him. "Gracias," he said and didn't utter another word for the entire shift.

Weeks later, it happened again. "I slept three hours last night. I need just one, para aliviarme."

"Really?"

"Please, Julio. It won't happen again, te lo juro." Again, I brought him a beer in a to-go coffee cup. Again, he gulped it down and performed every task without error or complaint.

I've lost count by now, but another Saturday brunch, another to-go cup. I strolled by the back area and saw it. The inside was crimson. Blood came to mind. His well-being concerned me. On second glance, I spotted granular red dots and ice cubes. He'd had the audacity to craft himself a michelada; the bright specks of Tajín were the giveaway. If he hadn't been such a stellar worker, I would have run him off.

Hay muchos pájaros, I thought. There are many birds. He didn't say which beer he wanted; he just said he needed one and that no birds should know about it. Not the hawks in the kitchen, and especially not the head hen up front, my tía.

The cooler was a few feet behind the register where Aunt Bobbie was taking orders. I'd have to wait until she became too busy to notice. Fifteen minutes later, the queue dwindled, and Aunt Bobbie went up front to bus a couple of tables. I had my chance. I reached for a beer and a to-go cup and placed them against the coffee mugs. When she went to the back to drop off dishes, I cracked open the beer and cascaded it into the cup. The pour was reckless, and the foam rushed to the top like in those beer commercials, head beyond the brim but not over.

Aunt Bobbie returned to wipe down the table she'd just bussed. While she was up front, I rushed back through the kitchen to deliver the cup. La niña was there, but she played dumb. I dropped the cup off and brushed my elbow against the prep as if to say, "Here's your beer. Don't make me regret this." He gave me a sympathetic look.

Later in the shift, I had time to check on him. "How was last night?" I asked.

"It was nothing," he said, ranchera music playing from his phone. I believed him. His eyes looked normal and not like they needed eye drops. "A cuate and I split an eighteen-pack, nine beers each. I was back home by one. I don't think I'm going out this weekend."

"You're not going out tonight?" I asked in disbelief.

"No. I'll be here until nine. I'll have my esquini, then go home."

I tilted my head.

"But that doesn't count."

Every Saturday, he'd ask la doña if he could make himself an esquini, a skinny margarita with no added syrup. He had blood sugar issues, so drinking an esquini seemed like the responsible thing to do.

After so many beer bottles, to-go coffee cups, and esquinis, surely the others must have known what was happening, but no one said a word. The birds didn't chirp.

# Jack

Sara, one of our cocineras, opened the backdoor just as we pulled into the parking lot as if she were waiting for us to arrive. Sara always greeted Mom using the formal usted, although she always used the familiar tú with me. "Did you remember to bring the brooms?" Mom asked. Sara went to her truck and pulled a pair of flat-edged shovels from behind the driver's seat. I keep confusing shovel and broom in Spanish. Escoba somehow sounded like shovel but meant broom. Pala was the word Mom said, the real word for shovel.

Sara placed both shovels on the ground next to me. 'Ten. ¡A trabajar!' She said with a smirk. I heard there is a word in German that means joy derived from the suffering of another. It was like that, only her joy was derived from watching me work.

A blanket of snow covered our patio and much of the parking lot, not sleet, but puffy snow, the thickest powder I'd seen in all my years in Texas. The meteorologists called it the worst winter storm Texas had seen in decades, a once-in-a-lifetime event. That morning, the streets were majestic, white everywhere, like the Christmas we all wished for as kids but never got. The magic was short-lived, however. Local infrastructure wasn't prepared for an Austin snow globe. The streets were too treacherous for many to navigate. Water pipes exploded. Worst of all were the state-wide power outages. The café was without electricity.

Power didn't return for another six days. By then, the streets were more or less navigable. Only the sections with little traffic or perpetual shade still had ice—including our patio. Now that we had power and would be re-opening soon, it was on me to shovel the winter away.

The front section of the patio was effortless. A simple swing of the shovel removed the snow without further negotiation. Between swings, I lifted the shovel and nudged the icicles that clung from the awning and lights above until they crashed down and shattered. Missing school on ice days as a kid came to mind.

I'd heard northern transplants carp about how much they didn't miss winter when they moved to Texas—winter boots, heavy coats, chained car tires. As far as I was concerned, shoveling snow was no different than raking leaves, only in the end, you had a snowman.

The most important section of the patio was the patch in front of the main entrance. I swung the shovel with the same efficient movement, only this time, the shovel swept the snow to one side, revealing a mammoth slab of ice. My next swing was less economical, intended to fracture the slab. The shovel stopped abruptly, and the recoil reverberated through my gloves straight to my neck and back.

The jolt forced me to change my strategy. My swings became vertical stabs, like digging post holes, but I only managed to remove small shavings of ice with each stab, which was quite demoralizing. By the end of the day, I'd be lucky to have enough shavings for a snow cone. Only a buffoon would frazzle and fray the cartilage in their neck and back on ice like this. Sara came to mind. Surely, she expected me to remove everything. Only a huevón would leave so much as a single flake anywhere on the patio.

A hooded man with a goatee wearing a trench coat approached. I'd seen his face for years. His name hung on the tip of my tongue. He worked at Quack's, the bakery a couple of doors down, sweeping the sidewalk, cleaning the windows, and directing the line of customers during Covid. For whatever reason, I never saw him behind the counter.

"Hey there," he said. "Looks like you have a lot on your hands. Wondering if I can help in any way."

"I think I have this under control. There isn't much."

"I'd love to help. Maybe you have an extra shovel or something, anything?"

"You know, I have another shovel if you really want to help."

"I'd love to, thank you." I fetched the extra shovel, and he got right to work. We had an unspoken plan. He shoveled the sidewalk while I shoveled the patio.

"So, how have you been these last few days?" I asked, thinking small talk would help the time pass.

"I'm okay. Had to leave my place. I'm just coming from the shelter."

"Oh. I'm sorry to hear that."

"It's okay. The shelter, I had to leave … It was overheating in there anyway."

"Really? It was *that* warm?"

The man stopped shoveling and looked at me with long, tired eyes. It wasn't the first time someone's humor was lost on me.

I bounced from section to section, crashing the shovel against the ice in muscled sprints. Soon, my scarf was too warm. Then my palms got moist, and my gloves came off. I glanced at the man and noticed that he worked at a steady cadence. A few minutes later, when I looked over again, he seemed to be using the shovel like a broom, sweeping the snow off the ice. He caught me watching him work.

"Easy there, young man. Lots of muscles you're probably not used to using."

"I'm good," I said dismissively.

"Gonna overheat like that, too." Yeah, said the man who uses the shovel like a broom, I thought.

I revisited a section that had been too hard to work on. Now, the ice was translucent; it sloshed over with a single swing. That explained why the man was sweeping the snow. He was moving the snow off the ice so the sun would melt it.

Sections of the patio were in the shade, so I revisited my old strategy and took a couple of hardy swings at the white ice. Two recoils was enough. The shaded ice was still hard as stone and too dangerous to leave. One of the patches was at the sloped entrance to the patio, the perfect place for someone to break a wrist and have their lawyer serve us paper.

When a red pickup pulled into the parking lot, I glanced up but continued to work until I heard the window roll down.

"Gonna open today, ay?" It was my friend Tony and his wife Erin.

"Oh, hey there! Y'all doing okay?"

"We're fine." He smiled. "You're using the right tool for the ice. And you know what works well, too? Salt."

"Really?"

"Yeah, and you don't need much, either. A little goes a long way."

I went inside and grabbed the kosher salt we used to rim our ritas. My friends were Yoopers from Northern Michigan. They knew a thing or two about cold weather.

Another regular passed by and saw me sprinkling salt. He mentioned pouring hot water over the ice. Neither of the two strategies worked instantly. But it was still morning. Soon, the sun would be directly overhead. I put the yellow 'wet floor' sign over the shaded ice and migrated to the last section, the front parking lot. The man with the other shovel joined me.

"You know, this is the first time I've had to shovel snow and ice," I admitted. "Nothing like this has ever happened."

"It hasn't happened while I've been here, but back home, it happened all the time."

"Where's home?"

"Chicago. One time, in the seventies, when I was still married, there was a massive pile of snow in the parking lot of a shopping center I frequented. It stayed there until June." We stopped shoveling and looked at each other. "Yeah, June. Can you imagine?"

"So, this is something you're used to?"

"Well, I wouldn't say that either. I've been in Texas for so long now."

The crescendoing sun made removing ice satisfying and therapeutic. Hard to say where the pleasure came from. Maybe from visible accomplishment, the way yardwork feels. Or it might have been the unfamiliarity that made it enjoyable.

"Does this remind you of home," I asked the man. "Is this nostalgic?"

"I think you got it," he replied, spreading imagined nostalgia to me.

Half the front parking lot was still covered in a benign layer of snow and ice. I swept the snow from one section while he chipped away at a patch of ice. I heard him say something to himself as he shoveled. As our sections got closer together, then met, I noticed that the man was singing to himself, though not loud enough for me to make out the lyrics. I used to work with a couple of guys who sang as they swept, mopped, and scrubbed the plancha. I usually couldn't make out their lyrics, either.

For months after that, I randomly bumped into the man who helped me. Sometimes, we reminisced about that frigid morning when we swept and shoveled snow and ice. For some odd reason, I thought his name was Harold. His name is Jack.

# Out of Grace

Much of the Spanish I learned traveled through my English lens first. And through that lens, the lavatrastes kept calling me "not gracious" or maybe "ungrateful." He looked over his shoulder before he said it in a low voice so no one else could hear: a special delivery only for me. He was obviously trying to cut me. I could tell by how he accented the word, snarled his nose, and punched out each syllable with his diaphragm.

Not knowing the meaning of desgraciado was an advantage. Not gracious, not grateful? What am I not grateful for? The lavatrastes could tell I had no idea what he was saying, and it made him laugh. The next time we worked together, he said it again. ¡Desgraciado! With an oomph on the ciado. Every time he said it, he rolled over in a robust laugh that was just as insulting, as though he was getting away with something, como un travieso, like a naughty child. No doubt he was trying to get a disgusted response from me. He got a reaction from me, alright, though not the one he hoped for. I wasn't disgusted. I was bewildered.

His hoots were impossible for the others to ignore. Once they found out, they joined in, too. The planchero and the line cook both started saying desgraciado, but in a different way. Their noses didn't lift or wrinkle when they said it. Their eyes didn't sharpen. I could still see the warmth in their cheeks. It was their way of poking fun. I paid no mind to the new trend. Reaction is the oxygen words beg to receive. Starve the flame of its fuel, and soon, the words will peter out.

Years later, when the lavatrastes was long gone, that word wiggled out of one of the many nooks in my head. I was at work that afternoon, and Monserrat was prepping for the evening rush.

"Oye. ¿Qué quiere decir desgraciado?" I asked her abruptly. What does desgraciado mean? She was not one to react without calculation. She grew pensive and silent, which made me think I might have crossed a line. "¿Es una palabra pesada?" I asked, trying to dampen the tense silence.

"Yeah, that's a bad word."

"Would people get into a fight over this word?"

"Algo así," she confirmed.

"How would you explain it?"

Without saying a word, her eyes fell into space. Her expression indicated that she was playing over various scenarios in her head, struggling to provide a clear example. "I don't know how to explain it," she finally said, "but it's a bad word."

Later that week, just after walking into work, I heard my name called. It was Papá. He was on the phone at his favorite booth in the corner near the restroom, combing over local real estate listings. He was no longer involved with the restaurant but still liked visiting.

While we were chatting, the question that had been knocking around my subconscious sprang to mind. "Hey, let me ask you something. To you, what does desgraciado mean? I'm pretty sure it's a fighting word, but what exactly does it mean when someone calls you that?" I didn't tell him or Mom that the lavatrastes had called me that many times. What use would it have been to burden them?

Papá paused, just as Monserrat had. "No. Calling someone desgraciado isn't a fighting word. If you call someone desgraciado, your finger better be on the trigger cause all hell is about to break loose. By the time desgraciado comes out, everyone is already acting like an animal." When Papá said "hell," he always meant it. He wasn't a violent man at all, but he's from Venezuela, arguably one of the most turbulent countries in the Western Hemisphere.

I went ahead and used the word in a sentence in hopes of capturing its true essence. "No, no, no," Papá interrupted. "You have to say it with character." He took off his glasses and put his phone down. From one moment to the next, Papá morphed into the villain from your favorite telenovela and delivered a string of obscenities. I noticed he accented the ciado part of desgraciado like the lavatrastes had. His performance made us both laugh. Don't ask which combination of words he strung together. Just know that the words he used were caustic, words I don't care to immortalize.

His answer wasn't exactly what I was looking for. I was hoping for a more literal explanation, something along the lines of someone without hope – someone who had forgotten how to say gracias, an unthankful person. That was how I wanted to understand it, a word I barely found offensive at all.

Like most offensive words, desgraciado can be interpreted in many ways. If you ask me, there was another meaning, one beneath the surface. Desgraciado can be used as a put-down, but it also reflects the person who says it. Imagine the misfortune someone must have experienced to make them step so blatantly out of grace with their words.

# They're Just Not For Me

Usually, Mom's defense strategy was airtight. This time, though, she slipped up. A marketer called the café and wanted to schedule a meeting. Without knowing who this person was or what the meeting was about, she said yes. And worse, she said that I would be the person attending the meeting the very next day, just after our lunch rush.

Many of the past cold calls we'd received had been blatant scams. One guy called and threatened to cut power from the business that afternoon if we didn't send money. He only spoke Spanish, which gave me the impression that he primarily targeted Hispanic-run businesses. There were women who called and rattled off like an audiobook on fast forward, also only in Spanish. The first few times I got those calls, I struggled and passed the phone to one of our bravas to iron them out. Eventually, I worked up the nerve to just hang up. Why Mom didn't do the same to this guy was beyond me.

The next day, we were swamped and backlogged in prep when a man in a green polo walked in and informed me of our two o'clock appointment. I got us both a beverage, and we went to the corner table on the patio, which Mom and I liked to use for intimate conversations.

He opened his pitch with a story about family-run businesses, probably thinking I'd sympathize with it. I did, not with his story, but with his effort and ability to spin a yarn. His story was tightly knit, with details he knew resonated with restaurateurs. I was aware that this was a sales pitch and that, more than likely, he was trying to sell me a service we didn't need.

Mom and I have the same problem, which is why this meeting was scheduled in the first place. For people who say yes for a living, saying no can be tough. It's easy to empathize with others, including marketers, like child-me watching the Discovery channel and crying when the gazelle was caught and eaten by the cheetah. Or if the gazelle sprang away, and the cheetah's cubs didn't eat, more tears.

He placed several sheets of paper on the table and started talking about pricing. He had a program in mind, an excellent fit for the business. I told myself to get up and leave. Just say no three times. That's how these guys are trained. If you say it once, they don't get it. You have to say it three times. No, no, no ... and I'm free. I didn't care how I came off or how he felt or if the cubs went to bed without supper. I told myself to stop feeling, stop thinking. Just *say it*.

Sara was halfway down the patio when I noticed her. The speed of her gait said it all: "Disculpa. Julio, the register won't open, and there's a line of people. I need you to come inside." She looked at the gentleman, "Sorry." Our point of sale hiccuped semi-regularly, though never had our POS failed so miraculously.

Trouble-shooting the sales system: Pull all the cords and reconnect them, reboot the tablet, check to see if the app is connected to the hardware properly. Perhaps the software needs to be updated. None of those things worked. I called tech support. Tech support put me on hold. Good, I thought. I'll put the marketer on hold, too.

Five minutes hadn't passed before the marketer walked up. "I'm thinking that maybe it's best if I swing by another time," he whispered.

"Thank you for understanding. I can't afford to have our system down."

The marketer was a man of his word. When he said, 'I'll swing by another time,' he meant it. A week and some change later, he returned wearing the same polo shirt. A true professional. "I was just in the neighborhood and thought I would check in with you again and see if we could schedule a time for another meeting?" *That's* when you say "No thank you" and hang up.

"Does right now work for you?" I asked. "I just have to wrap up a couple of things." He agreed. I offered him a drink, and before long, he had the same series of papers covering the table. I thought maybe I should hear what he had to say.

Somewhere in his pitch, I got sucked in and even found myself asking him questions like how he came up with the idea and how long he'd been in business. I was fascinated with his operation, not because it would increase traffic to the café, but because I thought his idea was clever. My anxiety about having to reject the marketer was replaced by curiosity.

He told a story about his longest-standing client, nearly twenty years, he claimed. The client had a restaurant in Round Rock, and he renewed every month. Because the strategy works, the green polo said. When he finished his story, I followed up with one of my own. Then one of his, later one of mine, like two sympathetic sparring buddies bobbing and weaving, yet refusing to lean into their crosses.

"So, what do you think? Is this something you and your mother would be interested in doing?"

"You know, I'll have to check with the boss. She's the one with the checkbook."

"Is there a time, perhaps, when the three of us could meet?"

"Well," I paused, "that's why I'm here, so she doesn't have to be."

"A few years ago," he said, "I want to say around 2015 or 16, I went into a dentist's office and had this same conversation with his assistant. The dentist was in the back of the office, doing something on the computer but still kind of listening, you know. I went on with the presentation, and as I explained how this differs from other programs, the dentist interrupted. He said, 'I've tried dozens of these programs, and none of them work. They're just not for me.' And he was right. There are so many garbage programs out there, they make the good ones look bad. Right?"

"Totally."

"Now, I had his attention," the man in the green polo simpered. "I asked him how many new patients come into his office. 'Often, when someone moves to a new home, they have to find a new doctor and dentist.' I told him that the last time I moved, I had to change my dentist, right? Which was a real shame because I liked my old dentist."

"'Eventually, I got an infection and had to find a new dentist.' I told him. 'And while the new dentist was working on me, one of his tools slipped and hit a nerve.' If that has ever happened to you, you know the feeling. No pain in the world like it. Just awful. I can see from his face that he knows exactly what that pain is like, and he says, 'I am sorry to hear that. Did you go back?' I said, 'I haven't gone to a dentist since. They're just not for me.' And he gave me this oh-you're-a-smart-ass look, which wasn't bad. He was from Boston or someplace up there. They love it when you talk back like that."

I laughed, and so did he. "It's the truth," he said. "The greatest obstacle I face is people's experiences with programs that suck. There are so many out there."

"You know, the dentist and my mom are opposites."

"How so?"

"Well, the dentist had tried everything, and nothing worked. My Mom hasn't tried anything, but her business works."

The crow's feet at the sides of his eyes smoothed out, though his smile remained mostly intact.

"But you know, let me check with her anyway. Tons of our regulars leave the area all the time. And considering our old-school style, this might work. I just need to talk with the boss first. Is there a business card in the envelope?"

"Didn't I give you one at our last meeting?"

"Oh, if you did, I'll ..."

"No, no. Don't worry." He pulled out his wallet and handed me a card. His shirt, envelope, and business card were all the same shade of green.

"Do you need a tea refill, one for the road?"

"I should be fine, thank you."

We got up and shook hands. He said that if he didn't hear from me in two weeks, he'd reach out again. "Sounds like a plan," I said.

As a courtesy, I emailed the marketer a couple of weeks after our meeting. He never messaged back.

# A Car Ride Home

Getting under a Latino's skin is easier than you think. Often, the same key that ignites his heart starts his car. You just need to remember two simple steps. First, ballpark the value of his whip. Then, with the most deadpan face you can muster, make him an unsolicited cash offer for twenty percent of the car's value. Let me tell you, few insults can compete. With a single stone, you call him both dull and broke.

These offers nearly always occurred in the parking lot over a post-work cigarette. Rogelio would open his wallet wide and low by his waist, in such a way that everyone smoking knew his net worth. He'd thumb through a wad of hundreds as if he'd been the recipient of la tanda that week. "How much for your truck?" he'd ask with feigned seriousness. In a single lick, he'd bedew his thumb and index finger and pull out two bills. "¡Ten! Now give me the keys." Everyone in the parking lot would break into synchronized laughter, including Rogelio himself.

Sometime later, as if from the same playbook, Alfonso approached me in the parking lot after work. "How much do you want for your camioneta?"

"No se vende," I replied. Not for sale.

"Te doy mil, así bien pagadito," he countered, offering me a thousand. No doubt Alfonso was trying to stick me in the ribs like Rogelio. Ever since I swapped out my Civic for a small truck, I got offers all the time. The serious ones were from car mechanics or random yarda guys who left notes under the windshield wipers. To top it off, my truck was a standard, a nonstarter for most people but not Latinos. Manual transmissions made them salivate more.

"If I sell it to you, what will I drive?"

"I don't know. You're from here. You'll find something, no problem."

"Lo siento." Sorry.

"Ándale!" he whined. "How much for la Poderosa?"

"What's wrong with your car?"

"It's not mine. It's my sister's. And it uses chingos de gasolina, eighty bucks every five days. ¡Imaginate!"

I could tell Alfonso was serious by how he said ándale and his nickname for my truck: La Poderosa, the powerful one. The not-so-serious offers nicknamed it El Podrido: the rotten one, like a furry strawberry.

Years later, a lavatrastes named Mauricio said "Julio vendeme tu camioneta." Sell me your truck. I asked him what I would drive if I sold my truck. He ignored me.

"¿Cuanto?" How much? I knew how this lowball game worked. I beat him to the punch and gave him a price three times the market value.

He turned his head away in disgust. "Neta Julio, how much for your truck?" His eyes were softer than the others when he asked about the truck. He didn't have a car and rode Capital Metro to work daily, which only took him half an hour. But after work, if one of his cuates didn't come for him, his commute home was nearly an hour via two buses. By comparison, my commute was between four and eight minutes, depending on the three traffic lights in between.

I asked Mauricio where he lived. North of the highway, he said, near all those really good taco trailers. Giving him a ride added fifteen minutes to my commute and took forty minutes from his. So, instead of selling him my truck, I offered to drive him home.

He was fascinated with the manual transmission and asked every possible question. "If you put the stick in the center, that's neutro?"

I nodded. "And if you push the clutch in, that's also neutro?"

Another nod.

The more he asked, the more I explained. He compared driving a stick-shift car to driving a motorcycle.

"Así es," I affirmed, without knowing anything about motorcycles.

Mauricio confessed that he wanted to learn to drive manual. "Sell me your camioneta, Julio."

"Siento mucho." I'm sorry. And I really was.

Now that I knew more or less where Mauricio lived, he wanted to know the same about me.

"Por alla," I pointed westward, over my shoulder. "Off Lamar."

He kept asking where, which cross street.

"Behind the bookstore."

He had no idea where the bookstore was.

"You know where the light and the gas station are?"

He nodded.

"Allí mero." My answers were intentionally vague. My apartment was nothing to be embarrassed about, at least not at the time. But I didn't want the guys from work to know where I lived.

Few were as persistent as Mauricio. He asked a few more times about buying my truck and many more times about manual transmissions. Our conversation about where I lived went the same way. He wanted to know how much I paid in rent. When I told him, he turned his head away with the same disgust he'd exhibited when I gave him a high counteroffer for my truck.

"I can't pay that."

"What's wrong with your place?"

"Nothing. I just need more space."

"How much do you pay?"

"Two fifty, everything included," he said. "But that's with four guys. Two in the bedroom and the other two en la sala."

It was as if he'd told me his cat died. There was no way I could say anything after hearing something like that. Mauricio knew his time there was borrowed. Eventually, he found a place a few blocks further north on the same street by the light and the gas station. That's where I dropped him off whenever I gave him a lift, not at his front door but at the gas station next to his complex. I asked if he liked his new spot and if he had more space. His arrangement was the same, two by two in a one-one.

As the months went on, we talked less. Mauricio used the ride to video chat with his esposa back home. It wasn't the most intimate setting, but since he lived with three guys in a one-bedroom apartment, his only private place was the toilet. The ambient noise from the road strained their conversations, but he's a persistent guy. He turned up the volume on his phone and spoke louder.

Mauricio moved up from lavatrastes to prep and then barman, but the video chats and phone calls in my truck continued. He even had the cojones to play music videos at full volume. How did I get roped into this? What began as a favor now felt like an obligation. Once, he asked if I could swing by someone's depa to pick something up before I dropped him off. When I asked what, he said money. Mauricio had lent money to a cuate and wanted to pick up the cash he was owed. I'm going to get into trouble doing this shit, I thought.

I wanted my fifteen minutes back. Then I remembered that it would take Mauricio an hour to get home. I thought I'd finally confront him about our rides one day, maybe ask for gas money or say I could only do it once a week.

One random afternoon, Mauricio rolled up to work, punched his card, and called me over.

"¿Qué pasó?"

"Ven," he said, nodding his head toward the backdoor. We went out to the parking lot.

"What do you think?" he said, waving his hands like a magician as he stood beside a gray Toyota sedan.

"Is this yours?"

"¡A huevo!" he said with a full-toothed grin. "I just bought it. What do you think?"

"Chingón."

"It's not standard. Pero ni modo. I still like it."

Getting a set of wheels is monumental, especially in the sprawl of Texas. I was happy for Mauricio, though I should have been happier.

In a bizarre way, I was kind of bummed about the car. Not because it wasn't manual, but because without warning, our after-work commute had come to an end.

# A Different Tool

As a kid, I used to ask Papá why he didn't open another restaurant. He claimed it was too risky, that to open a second restaurant, he'd have to risk the success of the first. He said something about it being too much work. At the time, his logic was beyond me.

After nearly two consecutive decades at the restaurant, it turns out that selling food is a hard dollar to earn. Which was precisely why Papá had other money-making strategies. If I had to summarize his method, I'd repeat one of his favorite sayings: "Take the money and run."

There was a time in the '90s when Papá operated a steam cleaning business out of a house he bought off Cesar Chavez, several blocks east of the highway. I can't recall which came first, the house or the business. The two were inseparable. The house had a peculiar smell, nothing I'd call home. He stored all his cleaning supplies there, as well as his personal non-everyday items, such as fishing poles and tools. There were two bedrooms. One was rented to a guy named Che, who helped Papà in the business and was a set of eyes he trusted to look after the house. Cesar Chavez wasn't the safest neighborhood then, nothing like it is today.

The steam cleaning business was short-lived, though not for lack of revenue. It was an explosive success. Paradoxically, the café had its own eruptions—bad ones. Relations between Aunt Bobbie and Papá were headed south to the point where Papá needed cash to buy her half of the restaurant. The only logical option at the time was to sell the power washing business to one of his friends and to sell the house on Cesar Chavez. Take the money and run.

Since opening another restaurant was out of the question, Papá poured his attention into other ventures, primarily real estate projects. I don't know what his search was like, but he eventually found another lot further north on the Eastside. I shouldn't say it was just a lot because there was a humble house on it. And by humble, I mean it had nearly collapsed. It wasn't the house that caught Papá's eye. It was the land he was after. He tore the house down and built another one.

That summer, when I asked if I could work at the café, he said no. Papá needed help at the construction site. One of the dumpsters on the lot was too full for the truck to haul away, so my job was to shovel garbage and debris from one dumpster to the other one. Once the dumpster was light enough to haul away, I helped mix cement for the crew laying the cinder blocks. I didn't care for the job. Mixing cement was vapid compared to the hustle and bustle of the lunch rush.

Many years later, Papá confessed that that was his favorite house. I agree. It had two large porches, one on the first floor and another on the second floor, with a spot for a hammock and a spectacular view of the Austin skyline, more specifically, an excellent view of the new Frost Tower, the tallest in town. The view of the tower was short-lived, however. Mom and Papá were on the rocks. What had been an investment became a short-term residence. Not long after, Papá had to sell the house. Take the money and run.

I never knew the details of each house. And by details, I mean the numbers. We didn't talk about how much he paid, nor did I know exactly how much he made when he sold. Those things didn't come up in conversations. Or if they did, I wasn't paying attention.

During Austin's real estate boom, Papá constantly told me we were near the top. He'd describe Austin real estate as "not having any meat left on the bone. Everything is so damn expensive," he'd say. He looked elsewhere and found Southeast Austin, an area of town that was still cheap. We called it the last frontier. Papá wasted no time sourcing a fixer-upper in Del Valle. He swore he would never build another house again. "Too much work," he said. Labor and materials were exceedingly expensive.

He lived in the Del Valle house and did his best to make it a home. We even spent one Thanksgiving there. The turkey was dry like it was every year, and the sides he served were not those we were accustomed to. The salad was different from the one Aunt Norma made. No Uncle Frank's green bean casserole, either. You know, the one with crispy onion bits on top. We were used to spending holidays with the entire family at Mamá Abuela's house where Mom and her family were raised.

There was nothing physically wrong with Papá's house. We had a good enough time whenever we were there, but it didn't feel like anything more than a house, never a home. We all knew that was how Papá made money. He found houses with plenty of meat still on the bone, put in the work, lived in the house for a bit, and then turned it around.

Houses that fit his formula were becoming scarce. People caught on to Southeast Austin, which drove up prices. "No meat on the bone," he'd repeat. He kept looking anyway until he found something else. It wasn't a house but a hefty tract of land many miles further out in no-man's land between Austin, Lockhart, and Bastrop.

To say that we discussed the idea would be too much. Papà did all the talking, and I listened. He planned to subdivide the land into one-acre lots, each with a prefabricated unit tarted up with a carport and a massive porch. The project was infinitely easier to describe than to execute.

The first unit he sold funded the second, the second funded the third, the third funded the fourth, and so on. He completed his project one at a time, living in each unit as he went along. By then, Mom and Papá were on good terms, so good that she lent him money when he ran dry. No bank would give him a loan.

We were accustomed to the way Papá did things. Not for a moment did I believe one of these units would become his home. Hell, even the word "house" was too much. When discussing his project, we used businessy words like "inventory" or "units." And every time he sold one of his units, he'd smile as if to say, "Take the money and run."

Around this time, Mom decided to put the restaurant up for sale, which brought me relief, especially when I thought of her. She worked Sunday through Sunday, with no days off. Even when she wasn't physically at the restaurant, she was still working. If she wasn't going to the accountant, she was going to the bank. If not the bank, to the store to pick up whatever. "It's always something," she would say. Selling the restaurant meant that Mom would finally get a much-deserved break.

I chewed on the thought. Solace and clarity soon faded away. Confusion flowed in.

The first few times Papá and I discussed the sale, he regurgitated, "Take the money and run." Not because he was insensitive, but that saying was his most familiar tool. He was in real estate and sold houses for a living. After making a sale, he went on to the next house and then the next. What does a father do but provide his son with the tools that work for him?

The café wasn't a piece of property with an early position. Nor was it a house in an up-and-coming neighborhood. The café felt more like a home. Certainly, it felt more like home than the place where I lived. I'd moved maybe once every three years or so. Only a few places in Austin still felt like they had when I was a kid. Mamá Abuela's house was one; the café was another.

I wasn't the only one who felt that way. Marisa and Luis lived out of town but stopped by the café whenever they came to Austin.

I wish I could romanticize their visits and say it was their first stop. It wasn't. Luis made it a tradition to go to Dan's Hamburgers right after landing. He'd come to the café for dinner. Marisa had a similar approach, though in reverse. The café was often her last stop before driving home, though she might stop by a time or two before that.

Other guests had similar habits. For a few, their welcome back to town was a visit to ours, sometimes with their luggage still in the trunk, even before they went home. I knew this because they often confessed it. It might be a couple returning from a vacation in Colorado or a grown child who ventured out of the nest for school or a first job. When they returned for Christmas or the summer, they always stopped in. Kids are still kids, at least to their parents and, in an odd way, to me. Now grown, they ordered the same things they had when they were years younger.

The day finally came. After nearly five years of trying, the contract was signed, the restaurant sold. There was a massive pulse of relief, followed by tears, then many iterations of sorrow and joy. The first tears were heavy ones that came from the chest, not the eyes. The tears didn't last because we had a river of work ahead of us. We had to get the new owners up to speed.

I talked to many people about the sale – customers, friends, and family. Eventually, I had a moment to sit down and talk with Papá. He was encouraging, and much of what he said was sincere. But he didn't use his favorite tool, he didn't repeat his favorite saying.